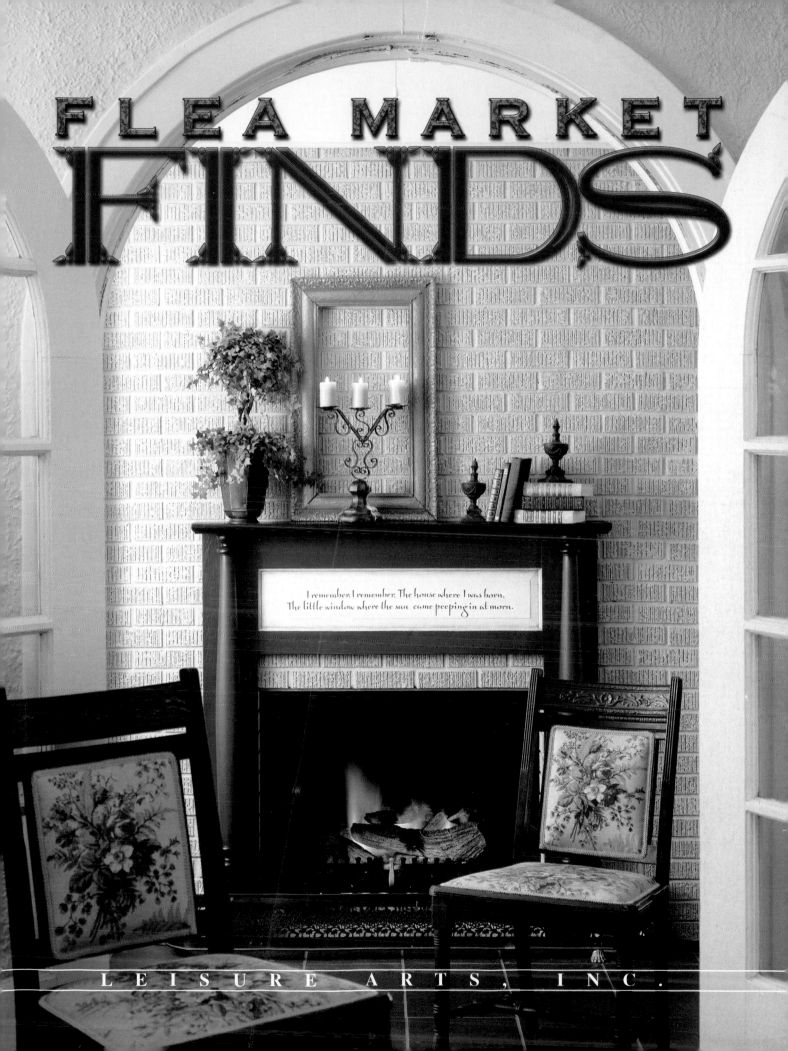

FLEA MARKET FINDS

I remember, I remember, The house where I was born,
The little window where the sun came peeping in at morn.

LEISURE ARTS, INC.

FLEA MARKET FINDS

A SPECIAL THANKS: *For the special contributions of four dedicated individuals, we offer our sincere thanks for making this exceptional book possible: Patti Sowers, for her incredible vision and creativity; Dale Rowett, for inspiring the wonderful presentation; Becky Charton, for showcasing our projects in such grand style; and Mark Mathews of The Peerless Group, for his beautiful photography.*

EDITORIAL STAFF
Vice President and Editor-in-Chief: Sandra Graham Case. *Executive Director of Publications:* Cheryl Nodine Gunnells. *Special Projects Design Director:* Patricia Wallenfang Sowers. *Graphic Artist:* Dale Rowett. *Director of Designer Relations:* Debra Nettles. *Publications Director:* Kristine Anderson Mertes. *Editorial Director:* Susan Frantz Wiles. *Photography Director:* Lori Ringwood Dimond. *Art Operations Director:* Jeff Curtis. TECHNICAL — *Managing Editor:* Leslie Schick Gorrell. *Senior Technical Writer:* Kimberly J. Smith. *Technical Writers:* Jean W. Lewis and Theresa Hicks Young. EDITORIAL — *Managing Editor:* Alan Caudle. *Senior Associate Editor:* Susan McManus Johnson. *Associate Editors:* Steve Cooper, Suzie Puckett, Taryn Stewart, and Linda Trimble. DESIGN — *Designers:* Cherece Athy, Lucy Beaudry, Polly Tullis Browning, Diana Sanders Cates, Peggy Elliott Cunningham, Amy Pritts, Anne Pulliam Stocks, Linda Diehl Tiano, and Becky Werle. ART — *Art Director:* Mark Hawkins. *Senior Production Artist:* Lora Puls. *Production Artists:* Elaine Barry and Ashley Carozza. *Color Technician:* Mark R. Potter. *Staff Photographer:* Russell Ganser. *Photography Stylists:* Sondra Daniel, Karen Hall, Tiffany Huffman, and Janna Laughlin. *Publishing Systems Administrator:* Becky Riddle. *Publishing Systems Assistants:* Myra S. Means and Chris Wertenberger. PROMOTIONS — *Graphic Artist:* Deborah Kelly.

BUSINESS STAFF
Publisher: Rick Barton. *Vice President, Finance:* Tom Siebenmorgen. *Director of Corporate Planning and Development:* Laticia Mull Cornett. *Vice President, Retail Marketing:* Bob Humphrey. *Vice President, Sales:* Ray Shelgosh. *Vice President, National Accounts:* Pam Stebbins. *Director of Sales and Services:* Margaret Reinold. *Vice President, Operations:* Jim Dittrich. *Comptroller, Operations:* Rob Thieme. *Retail Customer Service Manager:* Wanda Price. *Print Production Manager:* Fred F. Pruss.

Made in the United States of America

Library of Congress Control Number 2001099270
Hardcover ISBN 1-57486-245-6
Softcover ISBN 1-57486-246-4

10 9 8 7 6 5 4

CON

> All true civilization is ninety per cent heirlooms and memories — an accumulation of small but precious deposits left by the countless generations that have gone before us.
>
> — *Robert I. Gannon, S.J.*

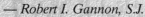

7 INTRODUCTION

8 FIRST IMPRESSIONS are lasting ones.
Guests will admire your novel use of flea market finds. Display a timely collection atop an easily restored shelf. Attach a "Welcome" sign to a vintage mailbox and use a wicker hamper as an umbrella stand!

TENTS

62 Collect vintage fabrics and linens to fashion cool **COTTON COMFORTS** for your home. Transform 1950's tablecloths into curtains with character. Create pillows from damask napkins and trim towels with found crochet!

76 A sewing machine cover, a table, a drawer, and a pair of well-traveled suitcases team up with plush fabric-covered foam cushions. The results are chic **OTTOMAN TRANSITIONS** with 5 prop-up-your-feet originals!

80 Want to make the best use of your space? **GET ORGANIZED!** Make a memo board from an old frame and a discarded drawer. Discover ingenious ways to employ vintage mailboxes, bins, tins, canisters, and more to stash your stuff.

90 Looking for **WONDERFUL WINDOWS** of opportunity? Easily transform archaic windows into a shabby-but-chic towel bar, a clever bulletin board, even a stunning stained-glass beauty! Proudly paint a Colonial-era American flag on a weather-worn window.

CONTENTS

Remember
your favorite,
flea market "find"?

Did it come at the end of a thrilling hunt? Or was it a bit of serendipity — a prize that seemed to drop out of the sky? For a lot of fans, flea market shopping is the chance to reconnect with the past and surround themselves with uniquely meaningful furnishings.

This book is all about the fun of unearthing treasures in the dusty booths and cluttered aisles of secondhand shops. It's about the "Eureka, I've found it!" joy of picking up a longed-for collectible at a bargain price. But mostly, it's about digging a little deeper and finding a second life for ordinary items that might otherwise be overlooked.

Leaf through these pages and you'll know right away what we mean. You'll see inexpensive resale items that have been transformed into useful, one-of-a-kind accents for your home. You'll also find great new ways to display your favorite collections. Some of our "Instant Ideas" are effortless makeovers you can finish in a flash. Others are "Weekend Wonders" that are ready in just a few hours. The best part? None of these projects requires special skills, so you're not stuck with drawn-out restorations once you bring your discoveries home.

So the next time you browse the tables of a tag sale, spare a second glance for the unimpressive items you usually pass up — they may be diamonds in the rough, just waiting for the perfect setting only you can provide!

First

To begin our mailbox transformation, we gently polished the box with a soft cloth soaked with brass cleaner, removing just enough tarnish to allow metallic highlights to shine through. We filled the box with moss-covered foam, ivy, and sprigs of flowers for color. The "welcome" sign hanging from the mailbox began as an old drawer front with a key lock. We brushed an uneven coat of paint over its existing finish, glued on two keys and our printed greeting, which can be found on page 155, then sealed the sign to protect it from the weather. For hangers, we threaded ribbons through eye screws installed in the top of the sign. This letter-perfect project can be ready to post in just one weekend!

Hampered by a surplus of umbrellas? Store them in a wicker hamper and save them for a rainy day! We left this basket unadorned, but some might benefit from a new fabric lining.

IMPRESSIONS

Because you never know when company's coming, you work hard to keep your home looking its best. How about giving your entryway an easy, do-it-yourself improvement that's also a first-class way to show your love of secondhand items? A good example is this wonderful old brass mailbox.

MAKE AN ENTRANCE

Greet arrivals to your front door with a bouquet of cheer! To hold your silk blossoms, use any container that appeals to you. We revived an old magazine basket by lining it with moss and covering its damaged areas with bits of glued-on moss. We then filled the basket with floral foam and added an array of color-coordinated flowers. For a balanced bouquet, remember to "pick" blooms of all sizes — small, medium, and large.

COLOR CONVENIENCE: Many craft stores display their flowers in color groups, making it easy for you to coordinate your selections to match your door or entryway.

start a
sparkling
conversation

The conversation's sure to be lively when your guests are greeted with a dish-lined walkway or twinkling candles and vases swaying in the breeze. To make a charming flower-bed border in an instant, search garage sales and junk shops for mismatched china plates. Don't worry if they're cracked, chipped, or broken … just "plant" the blemished edges in the soil!

Hang these beaded bottles and jars on your front porch or beneath an arbor. They'll hold fresh flowers or candles, giving your home extra sparkle both day and night. Turn to page 132 for the how-to's.

FOYER COMFORT

To put guests at ease, you need more than a simple welcome mat in your entryway. These attractive foyers get their appeal from inviting tables-turned-benches. They are graceful transitions you can easily achieve!

OPPOSITE: In just one weekend, you can bring a classic coffee table into the twenty-first century with a coat of fresh paint. To complete its transformation into a comfy bench, you need two kinds of coordinated padding. For the bottom, stack several layers of quilt batting on the tabletop. Cover the batting with a piece of fabric and glue the fabric to the edges of the table; then glue trim along the edges.

TIPS FOR SITTING PRETTY:
Replace glass or other fragile tabletops with plywood, and remember to test your table for sturdiness before you begin its makeover.

For the top cushion, simply cut a piece of thick foam to fit the top of your table. Wrap fabric over the foam gift-wrap style, overlapping the raw edges underneath and safety-pinning the fabric in place. We thought this classy new bench deserved a tufted cushion. To do this, we sewed through the foam in several evenly-spaced places, attaching a covered button at the top and a flat button at the bottom. At each tuft, we pulled the sewing thread taut to cinch the cushion.

ABOVE: Instantly convert a rattan end table into a cozy seat by wrapping decorator fabric around foam and plywood cut to fit your tabletop. Staple the fabric to the bottom of the wood for a quick, no-sew fix-up. To make your little bench the best seat in the house, top it with coordinating pillows.

REFLECT

REFLECT

Let your home reflect your sense of style — decorate the entryway with appealing items that have caught your eye over the years.

Greet guests with a display of petite timepieces. After ticking away the years in solitary service, each of these little flea market clocks found companionship as part of a well-loved collection. The coatrack they rest upon was either the mirrored top of an aged hutch or a piece from an old mantel. Whatever its former life, only minor modifications were needed to prepare it for new duties. Turn to page 133 to learn how this transformation took place in just a few minutes.

If you want to add grandeur to a simple arrangement, as on this hall table, use an empty ornate frame to emphasize a diminutive decoration. The large frame that borders the small mirror was restored to gleaming condition with a little rub-on gold wax finish. Keep an open mind to the possibilities and trust your instincts. Instant decorating success is guaranteed when you outfit your entryway in the best of all styles — your own!

Need a little help with your entertaining? Don't overlook the ever-faithful tray. To create this beautiful serving piece from a kitchen cabinet door, turn to page 133. It's a great example of how a flea market find can become an instant and indispensable asset.

TRAY

C H I C

PRETTY. PRACTICAL.

Imagine the cool thirst-quenchers these icy crystal pieces can serve! But without the hammered aluminum tray, the graceful glassware wouldn't seem half as tempting. Seek out a tray like this one to create a nostalgic refreshment center of your own. Pretty and practical can form the perfect union … again!

While America was recovering from the wartime efforts in the 1940's and 1950's, hammered aluminum became the beautiful and inexpensive material of choice for wedding gifts. These aluminum heirlooms are plentiful as resale items today.

Dance Lessons @ 4:00

Take note of this pretty and practical message center! Chalkboard paint transformed the bottom of a metal tray into a writing surface. For the hanger, a piece of folded fabric was threaded through the filigree border and fastened with a pair of clip-on earrings. In an instant, you've got a new way to post your important communiqués.

W ell-traveled trays are a fixture at most flea markets. You'll find them in all sizes, shapes, and colors, made from wood, metal, fiberglass, and more! Some have splendid pasts, while others have more humble beginnings, coming from the five-and-dime stores of the 1940's and later. Whatever their origins and present conditions, trays can be easily remade into useful and decorative items.

TOP: This round metal tray is a chic charmer created by placing it atop a small wooden accent table — that we turned upside down! To give the fairly new tray some age-old character, we applied paint and a crackle medium (see page 134).

RIGHT: On a metal tray that formed the top of a simple wooden table, we created a sleek leopard print using an easy technique you'll find on page 134.

Who would believe this French-inspired clock began as a fab-Fifties metal tray, grabbed up for a mere $3.00? Using the reverse side, we découpaged the rim with early 20th-century advertisements and a new clock face, à la Paris! A battery-powered clock kit and special longer hands complete this weekend wonder. See page 135 for the how-to's, then photocopy the clock face on page 151.

ROUND TRAYS
3ways

Romancing

In a world of fast-paced days and ever-changing trends, it's nice to know there's a place you can go for constancy and quality ... your home. Because your residence is the tangible outgrowth of your personal taste, you surround yourself with things that have special meaning to you — furnishings that help you enjoy your prized leisure hours.

Browsing through the next few pages, you'll find new ideas for using pieces of the past to enrich your life. And since you do live in a high-speed world, it's nice to know that many of these projects can be completed in an instant!

THE ✺ HOME

I remember, I remember, The house where I was born,
The little window where the sun came peeping in at morn.

I remember, I remember, The little window where the sun

I remember, I remember, The house where I was born,
The little window where the sun came peeping in at morn.

The house where I was born, came peeping in at morn.

— Thomas Hood

Express your sentimental side with a freestanding mantel that's eye-catching as well as thought-provoking. A quote from Thomas Hood's popular 1826 poem captures the spirit of nostalgia.

For a striking complement to the fireplace, give a pair of antique straight-back chairs a new glow with just a touch of matching paint and stain. The seating gains even more rapport when reupholstered in coordinating fabric.

Who would have guessed that a trip down memory lane could be so inviting? Or that these wonderful furnishings could be completed in just one weekend? See page 135 for our simple instructions.

I remember, I remember
The little window where th

Private
RETREAT

More than just a place to sleep, your bedroom is a private retreat … a place to "get away from it all." This tempting place of repose began with a headboard and footboard purchased at a garage sale. The original finish had been marred by years of use, but the inset panels and stylish sturdiness of these hardwood pieces gave them great project potential. See page 136 to work your own weekend recovery miracle. There's only one drawback to living in so much luxury — you may become a little reluctant to get out of bed in the mornings!

Gold is for the very wealthy — or the very wise flea market shopper! Filigree accessories that were a mainstay of well-dressed powder rooms in the 1960's are plentiful at secondhand sources. A quick application of metal leaf in the new variegated red tone, swirled with the colors of gold, coppery red, and bronze, gave this tarnished bath set the Midas touch. Follow the manufacturer's instructions to apply gold leaf adhesive and sheets of metal leaf to any surface that needs a little "24-karat" opulence.

To replace the face in the newly gilded clock, we cut a piece of foam-core board to fit the opening. After painting a base coat, we sponged the clock face with two coordinating paint colors. Two pairs of ornate earrings mark the numeral positions, while an easy-to-install pendulum clock kit keeps time with regal style.

Splendor in the Bath

KEEP IT EASY:
Before applying adhesive, remember to mask or remove the surfaces you don't wish to gild, such as mirrors or waste can liners. This little precaution will save you lots of clean-up time.

OPPOSITE:
We've gilded the clock, fingertip towel holder, and guess what else — it's a cover to disguise a can of hairspray!

Private, FIRST CLASS

Outfit your own private spa with your "found" treasures! With just a little planning, you can add comfort and convenience to your day while surrounding yourself with first-class style.

These privacy-giving tab-topped curtains originally were linen place mats. To make each panel, we joined two place mats, "stitching" through the holes in their open-work edges with narrow ribbon and weaving the ribbon ends to the back. For the tabs, we cut equal lengths of wide ribbon and folded them in half. Using a button on each, we sewed the tabs to the top of the panel, spacing equally and stitching through all the layers.

Use a hand cart to keep bathing necessities within easy reach. This old-fashioned tea trolley only needed silver spray paint to restore its former glory. Once your cart is ready, you'll still have time to spoil yourself with your favorite bath elixirs and potions, because both the cart and the curtains can be finished by Saturday night!

NEW GLAMOUR FOR OLD GLASS

TOILETTE DE LA MER	TOILETTE DE LA MER
Shampoo	Conditioner
PARIS	PARIS
TOILETTE DE LA MER	TOILETTE DE LA MER
Lotion	Bath Oil
PARIS	PARIS

THE FRENCH CALL THEM objets trouvés, OR "FOUND OBJECTS." WE KNOW EXACTLY WHAT THEY MEAN. THESE vintage vessels WERE ONCE GARAGE-SALE BARGAINS. SILVER PAINT ON THEIR LIDS AND STYLISH STICKERS MADE THEM BRAND-NEW BATHING BEAUTIES — in an instant! PHOTOCOPY OUR LABELS TO ADD DISTINCTION TO YOUR OWN BOTTLES OF "BUBBLY."

Your bedroom should be the most comfortable — and comforting — space in the house. Dress your bed with plump pillows and soft linens, making it a cozy spot to relax. For an unexpected touch of romance, convert a wire-mesh fireplace screen into a wall-mounted headboard with fabric-covered panels. See page 136 for the easy instructions. And while you're in the makeover mode, why not complete several sets of the panels in fabrics to change with the seasons? You'll have the time, because this easy project can be completed in a weekend — or less!

Fresh flowers are a lovely indulgence! Nestle sweet-smelling roses in a gleaming porcelain teapot at the bedside.

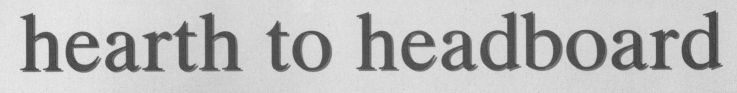

hearth to headboard

TIP: *To center your wallpaper scenes, use a single layer of tissue paper to cut a pattern slightly smaller than the area to be covered. You'll be able to see the motif through the tissue paper as you mark the wallpaper for cutting.*

This battered wooden tray is totally refreshed in its new role as a provincial mirror. We applied new paint to the areas the mirror would not cover, then sanded the paint to give it a distressed look. Silicone adhesive holds our secondhand mirror in place, while strips of pre-pasted wallpaper (see Tip, opposite) form the border on the rim of the tray.

take the
scenic
route

*f*or centuries, pleasing pastoral scenes graced decorator fabrics used for everything from sofas to curtains, but *toile de Jouy* isn't just a patterned fabric anymore. All of these flea market beauties got their new vistas from wallpaper. After painting the furniture, we cut pre-pasted wallpaper pieces (see Tip, opposite) to cover selected areas. We moistened and smoothed the wallpaper into place and added new drawer pulls to the dresser. In just a weekend, these secondhand furnishings gained marvelous new horizons!

spice
OF
life

*Season
your days
with
romance!*

Instead of passing up old silver salt and pepper shakers at the flea market, buy them to use as dainty miniature vases. For an instant centerpiece, arrange them on a doily-topped cake stand hung with prisms. And don't toss the shaker lids — they're tops as caps for ornate tassels to adorn window shades, lamps, doorknobs, and more!

FANCY THIS: It's easy to give a ready-made tassel a dash of true elegance. Old pieces of costume jewelry are ideal for adding sparkle — choose necklaces or dangling earrings like the one on this key tassel. Layer on the richness with woven trims. Glue the lid from a silver salt shaker onto the top of the tassel and thread matching embroidery floss through 2 holes in the lid to make a hanger. Your tassel is transformed into a tasteful bit of ornamentation!

Beautiful MEMORIES

The real value of our favorite treasures is in the memories they evoke. To display your timeless keepsakes, consider recycling a wire-mesh fireplace screen into a vanity mirror. Items that seem unrelated to each other — old keys, a fancy drawer pull, little perfume bottles, and a floral cone — gain unity from a large central mirror and the simple lines of the screen. Use jewelry pieces for dressy hangers and weave the ends of a satin bow through the wire mesh to fashion a border along the top. Add a couple of meaningful photos and your heartwarming collection is complete.

ABOVE: Gather pearls from old jewelry and attach them to a candle using gold craft pins or by softening the wax (see page 137). Display in a memorable dish. Beautiful!

BATHING

BEAUTY

For these instant indulgences, search your cabinets and comb secondhand stores for white ware & little luxury linens.

What could be more fetching than a trayful of pamper-me pretties, positioned to catch the eye?

Fill an ivory vase or pitcher with brushes.

Treat yourself to vanilla-scented candles in tiny teacups — guaranteed to be soothing!

Toss soaps and seashells into a scalloped salad bowl.

For splendid hand towels, roll up gently aged dinner napkins and display them in a shallow urn.

Pour bath salts into a gravy boat, then sprinkle spoonfuls of the fragrant crystals into a tub filled with warm water.

Now, settle in for a restful soak. With all the time you saved on these easy bath ideas, you can linger as long as you like.

Waxing elegant

*E*verything looks more *beautiful by candlelight,* so it makes sense to give your pretty pillars the setting they deserve. For holders that reflect all this loveliness, try a mix-and-match approach to stacking crystal plates with silver trays and dishes. Leave your pristine pillars unadorned or soften their effect in an instant with romantic bows and roses.

OPPOSITE: As you search for candleholder components, don't limit yourself to tableware — the sparkling glass bowl on a painted candle stand is actually a globe from a light fixture. Once your pillar is in place, add more glow around its base with strands of costume jewelry — you've got razzle-dazzle radiance in an instant!

enlightened

ideas

As the focal point of a reinvented lamp, your treasures will get renewed respect. Scout tag sales for the perfect lamp base and lampshade to highlight your favorite possessions or flea market finds. We've lost count of how many pretty, practical, and downright playful combinations we've discovered this way.

A display lamp kit makes a pleasant perch for a ceramic collectible like our rooster. Paint or stain the wooden base included in the kit and glue a fabric-covered circle of cardboard on top. Look for the perfect vintage shade while you roam flea market aisles, then embellish it with braided raffia trim. The finial is a speckle-painted egg glued on a raffia "nest."

ABOVE: See page 138 to make a tempting topiary lamp using an assortment of resale items and easy-to-use craft supplies.

> **DON'T BE "A-FRAYED":**
> *An easy way to mend a frayed electric cord is to use a quick-wiring plug. Just follow the manufacturer's instructions to cut off the damaged area and insert the cord end into the plug.*

Stir a little sweetness into your day with a petite sugar-bowl lamp! Make a floral-foam base inside the bowl, then glue a candlestick lamp and sheet moss to the foam. For the matching fabric-covered shade, follow the directions on the facing page and add a bit of fringe. The results are *pure delight!*

COVERING A SHADE

Whether your lamp was created from your own imagination or found at a flea market, the shade is essential for that "perfect touch." Craft shops, home centers, and lighting stores carry a variety of choices from modern styles to vintage replicas. You can even buy self-adhesive shades to cover with your own fabric or paper. If your found shade simply needs recovering, follow our easy instructions and your "new" lamp will be "made in the shade."

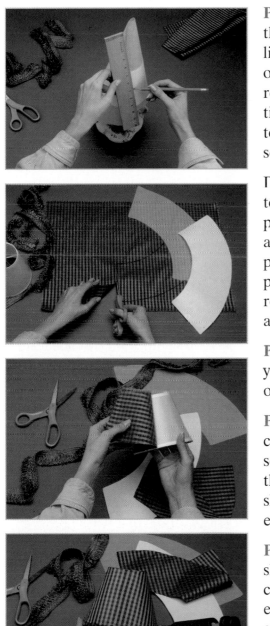

PHOTO 1: To make a pattern to cover a basic shade, find the seamline of the shade or use a ruler to draw a vertical line from the top edge to the bottom edge. Place one edge of a piece of tissue paper along the seamline and use removable tape to hold it in place … wrap the paper tightly around the shade and tape to secure. Use a ruler to draw another vertical line on the paper, 1" beyond the seamline for the overlap.

Draw lines along the top and bottom edges of the shade to complete your pattern. Leaving the first edge of the paper taped to the shade, untape the overlapping edge and finish drawing lines along the top and bottom of the paper. Remove the paper from the shade and cut out the pattern along the drawn lines. Check the pattern by replacing it on the shade and make any needed adjustments.

PHOTO 2: Draw around the pattern on the wrong side of your fabric and then cut the cover from the fabric. Press one short end of the cover ½" to the wrong side.

PHOTO 3: Apply spray adhesive to the wrong side of the cover. Beginning with the unpressed end along the seamline and aligning the top and bottom edges, center the cover on the shade; gently ease the cover around the shade, adhering it to the shade and smoothing toward the edges. Glue the pressed end in place.

PHOTO 4: Adding a matching decorative trim to the shade covers the raw edges and gives it a finished look … cut a length of trim to fit along the top and/or the bottom edges of the shade; beginning and ending at the seamline, glue the trim in place. If you do not want to use a decorative trim, cut your pattern and fabric slightly larger at the top and bottom, and glue the raw edges to the inside of your shade after you have the cover in place.

light repast

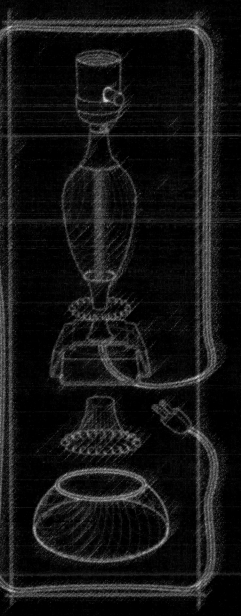

The light-and-easy recipe for these tasteful illuminations is just a few minutes of your time and a pinch of imagination. Spread a glow at your next feast with towering crystal lamps. Ours arise from gluing a petite boudoir lamp atop a stack of sparkling glass bowls and candleholders, securing each piece with clear-drying epoxy. For the fanciest of finials, top off your lampshades with lids from candy dishes.

New lampshades are a quick trick to update the look of any lamp, especially when you glue beaded trim to the edges. If your beading has an unfinished binding that shows, conceal the binding with braid or other decorative trim.

YOUR JUST DESSERTS: A silver-plated, three-tiered canapé tray can easily take on the task of spotlighting your prettiest cookies. Simply attach a C-clamp-style light socket onto the tray's handle and add an embellished lampshade.

SIMPLY SOPHISTICATED: *A discarded architectural column is the basis for an elegant floor lamp; top it with a sleek trumpet shade you've ornamented with gently worn jewelry and hat flowers. See page 138 for complete instructions.*

FAVORITE COLUMNS FOR *light reading*

I't's that perfect time of the evening … dinner's finished, the dishes washed and put away, the worries of the day forgotten for the moment. You're ready to pour a cup of tea, settle into your favorite chair, and enjoy a little light reading. Why not illuminate your hideaway with one or two designer-look lamps!

NATURAL CHARM: *For a casual corner, turn to page 138 to make this apple-studded topiary lamp using a candlestick lamp base.*

Romancing the Chandelier

There's a rags-to-riches story behind this charming chandelier. The original fixture was antique brass — a relic of the Early American decorating trend of the 1970's. Over one weekend, we updated its look by sponging cream-colored paint over the brass surfaces and adding glass prisms and strings of pearly beads. Softened by bow-embellished miniature lampshades, this Cinderella ceiling fixture has reached a new height of feminine style!

Glue a pretty bow and crystal prism to each shade. Pearl-trimmed braid, glued to each bobeche, offers hanging loops for more of the glass teardrops. Like lots of sparkle? Use narrow ribbon to tie on additional prisms.

hat's
a pretty
lamp
shade

TOP THIS! We used silk flowers and the veil from an ultra-feminine hat to give old-fashioned flair to a purchased lampshade. Delicate lace, once the edging on a pillowcase, encircles the lampshade's rim. The milk glass lamp base only needed primer and paint on its wooden parts to make the whole lamp look light and airy.

FINESSE WITH FINIALS: From whimsical to elegant, give a crowning touch to any lamp by attaching your own embellishments to its original finial or to various-shaped finials from the hardware store. Use small ceramic figurines, a tiny bottle, toys, chess pieces, wooden shapes — anything goes. A clip-on earring tops our Column Floor Lamp (close-up, page 55). Let your imagination take light!

Most home improvement centers, hardware stores, and craft shops stock lamp components that can help you transform your flea market treasures into delightful one-of-a-kind lamps – the quick and easy way! Lamp fixtures, sockets, wiring, and bases are available in electric or battery-powered versions.

$\mathscr{P}$RETTY IS...

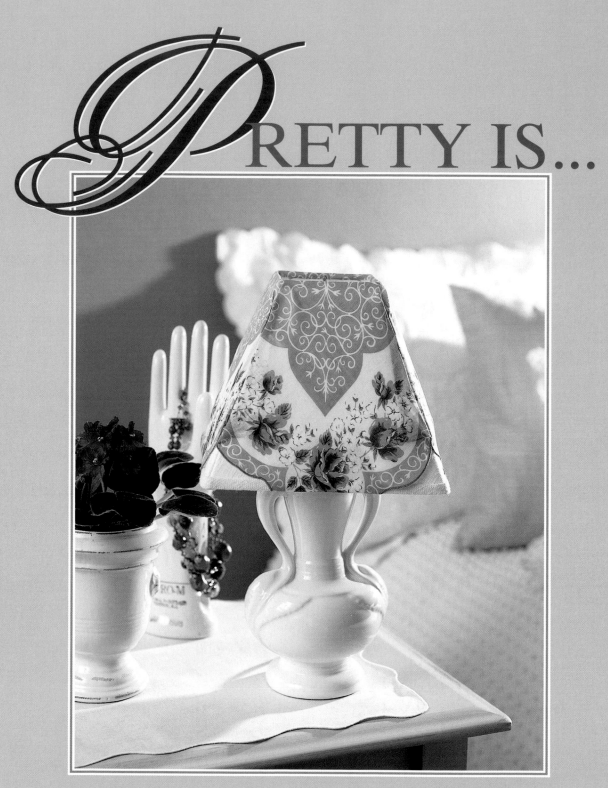

If nostalgia brings a tear to your eye, you might want to have vintage hankies in hand when you revisit yesteryear. Floral-print handkerchiefs are instant pick-me-ups for little lampshades. Best of all, a coordinated grouping of these dainty delights can be ready in just an hour or so!

*A small, plain shade
blossoms in an instant
with a delicate handkerchief
cover. Just cut the hankie in half
and press a hem along the cut
edges. To gather, thread a needle
with narrow ribbon and sew a
running stitch near the hemmed
edge of each piece, leaving long
ribbon ends. Draping both halves
of the hankie over the shade, tie
the ribbon ends into a bow at
each side.*

*A teacup or a tiny vase is a
feminine base for one of these
dainty lampshades. Simply
position a battery-operated
candlestick lamp securely
in your collectible and fill in
around the candlestick with
pearls, moss, or silk
flower petals.*

AS PRETTY DOES

To cover a square shade with a handkerchief, drape the hankie over
the shade, centering the handkerchief points at the shade's bottom
edges. Pin the hankie along the top of the shade and make inverted
pleats along each corner of the shade — smooth the handkerchief
flat against the lampshade sides, adjusting the pleats as necessary and
gluing them in place. Leaving pins in place, carefully cut the center
from the hankie about ½" inside top edges of shade. Glue the cut
edges of hankie to the inside top of shade and, if necessary, glue the
handkerchief points to the inside bottom of the shade.

cotton
COMFORTS

Collectible linens have timeless appeal. For some of us, the hand-crocheted borders of old-fashioned pillowcases evoke memories of Grandma's house or perhaps a weekend spent at a cozy bed-and-breakfast inn.

These projects are great ways to use vintage pillowcases that might otherwise languish in a drawer or closet. And some linens are so pretty, you'll just want to fold them nicely and lay them out for show!

Consider purchasing less-than-perfect linens with elaborate or highly detailed borders or edgings. These will yield the most decorative impact on your makeover projects — and they can be found at bargain prices because of their stains and signs of wear.

A pair of pretty pillowcases can bring a coordinated look to redecorated room accessories such as our waste can and chair (opposite). We used the end of one case to create the simple chair back cover. The matching case made a dainty apron for a waste can that we spruced up with fabric-covered poster board. Instructions for both projects are on page 138.

Whether handed down through the family or selected at a secondhand shop, linens are little luxuries that never go out of style. The vintage pieces are ideal for creating decorative accents that offer a hint of Victorian flair.

Little Linen Luxuries

Gussy up a miniature dress form in flea market style. Outfit it with pretty pieces from antique handkerchiefs, collars, and crocheted doilies. Add embroidered flowers and leaves cut from vintage linens, then adorn it with dangling necklaces of tiny pearls. Further embellish your perfectly feminine curio with lacy trims, rhinestone buttons, and costume jewelry reclaimed from the past.

Synonymous with elegance and comfort, linen touches every element of our lives. It was a mainstay fabric for our ancestors and, because of its beautiful durability, linens in pristine condition will still be around for our children to enjoy. For pieces already damaged by time and wear, however, the good portions can be salvaged to grace new creations.

ABOVE: Usually found in sets of four, napkins become an instant pair of lovely pillows. To fashion one of these simple pillows, pin together two damask napkins, matching wrong sides and edges. Using two strands of embroidery floss, work a running stitch about 1" from the edges all around, leaving an opening for stuffing. Insert fiberfill, then stitch the opening closed.

LEFT: Add a personal touch to a ready-made pillow with a corner cut from an embroidered linen cloth. Press and fuse raw edges to the wrong side, then sew antique buttons along the top edge to tack flap to pillow.

VINTAGE *Embellishments*

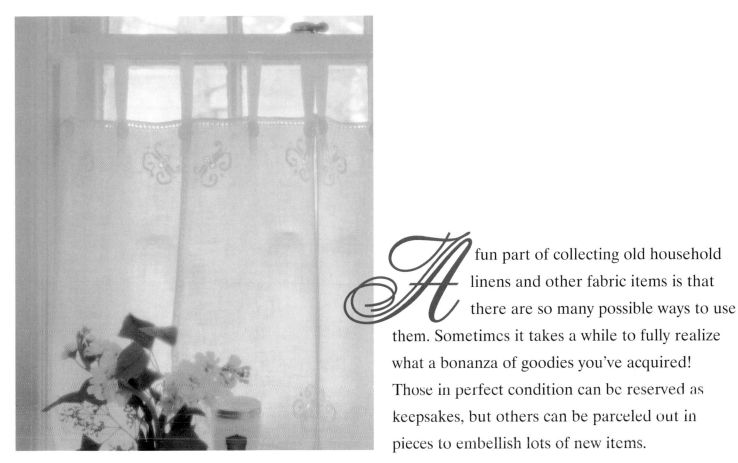

A fun part of collecting old household linens and other fabric items is that there are so many possible ways to use them. Sometimes it takes a while to fully realize what a bonanza of goodies you've acquired! Those in perfect condition can be reserved as keepsakes, but others can be parceled out in pieces to embellish lots of new items.

Options for reusing linens and lace are plentiful. You can trim hand towels with crocheted edgings or woven lace that you find in strips (or you can remove lace from an unusable cloth or garment). Also, you can transform place mats into curtains with ribbon tabs — instructions for these breezy window dressings are on page 33.

A favorite redo of ours is adding a section of an embroidered linen to a luxurious bath towel. The beautiful border shown opposite came from an old pillow slip with a crocheted edging (see instructions on page 139). For extra luxury, we added more lace in the seam between the towel and the border.

BEAUTIFUL

MORNING

Y ou'll wake up feeling pampered when your bedroom is lovingly adorned with beautiful collectibles. To make breakfast in bed more carefree, we dressed our tray with a spill-proof doily — it's a paper photocopy that was découpaged and sealed for protection (see page 140 for the simple steps). Trays in need of refurbishing are readily available at flea markets, along with china tea sets and vintage napkins like ours.

Bits of fancy crochet can be displayed like little works of art. To lend a feminine air to a room, glue an old-fashioned sachet onto a framed cutwork scrap. Or frame a portion of a pretty pillowcase or table scarf and border it with lace and buttons.

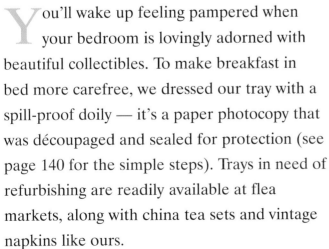

Remembrance

Add a personal touch to your address book and journal using snippets cut from a lace doily or pretty hankie. If your book has a printed cover, don't worry! Simply glue card stock over the printed area. Turn to page 141 for the complete instructions.

Every sentimental soul counts herself lucky if she chances upon a bundle of romantic notes and letters carefully tied with ribbon — cherished memories of times past. Make your own correspondence just as unforgettable with handcrafted notes. Color photocopies of vintage linens enliven these purchased cards and envelopes. See page 141 to create your own paper mementos.

Family photos and antique linens come together to form a charming link to the past. The cloth overlay on this ready-made album was cut from an embroidered pillowcase. Page 141 has the easy instructions.

Use tablecloths to dress a window with no-sew ease! For each curtain, fold the short end of a tablecloth over a tension rod and secure with safety pins. Tie back the curtains with ribbons. For the perky valance, no rod is needed! Just fold a tablecloth into a triangle and use ribbons to tie the triangle ends to nails. The window seat is cushioned by a piece of foam rubber wrapped in another tablecloth from yesteryear. Safety pins hold the cloth in place.

Red gingham ruffles add country zing to this flowered balloon shade. The cheery window treatment began as a vintage tablecloth. For how-to's, turn to page 141.

Sweet serendipity! We found our lily-print hankie and the orange-and-blue bonsai picture on the same shopping trip. With just a little hand sewing and four clear buttons, the handkerchief brightens a ready-made pillow.

Accents made from cheers gone by

Love the look of linens bedecked with bold flowers? Make use of these cotton-soft "bouquets" just as you would real blossoms gathered from your garden — arrange and rearrange them until the composition pleases your eye.

Haven't any floral-print linens? Search bazaars and resale shops for the vivid hues that were plentiful in years gone by … you never know when something stunning will crop up!

COTTON COMFORTS

Be an original! Transform your flea market bounty into artsy reflections of the real you. Cut loose. Go fancy free. After all, it's okay to color outside the lines once in a while! Put things together that don't usually go together. Refine your look with fabrics and finishes that are a bit off the beaten path. There's a method to your "mod-ness" — and it's whatever suits your whim and fancy.

HAVE YOU GONE MOD?

The far-out fabrics favored by a hip generation are fun to find and fashion into colorful cushions. These inviting floor pillows can't help but call attention to themselves!

They're easy to sew from flea market upholstery samples. Matching right sides and leaving an opening for turning, simply sew two squares or rectangles together. Clip corners and turn right side out. Stuff with fiberfill and sew the opening closed. For a funky finish, sew brush fringe into the seams when making the pillow.

Don't feel restrained by convention. When it comes to creating extraordinary things from flea market finds, there are no hard and fast rules!

Bring back the exciting Sixties *with an easy-to-spot metal TV tray, a relic from the days of* Laugh-In *and* Mod Squad*! Make it your own creation with a paint trick that involves using several colors of paint and round stickers in a variety of sizes (instructions on page 142). When your project is "right on the dot," remove the stickers to reveal an eye-grabbing pattern with layers of color. You'll have a unique piece of Americana that reflects a free-spirited decade!*

OTTOMAN TRANSITION

*Combine a crisply tailored foam cushion with
a vintage sewing machine cover, a suitcase,
and an occasional table to achieve a variety
of ottoman styles — from whimsical to elegant!*

See instructions on page 142.

The simple addition of a cut-to-fit foam cushion can turn a wooden sewing machine cover into an attractive and versatile ottoman (opposite). See page 142 to cover your cushion with the upholstery fabric of your choice. After the cushion is secured in place, consider adding easy-to-apply upholsterer's nail-head trim from the fabric store. What a tasteful transition!

Any end table with a flat surface can become a comfy parking spot for weary feet (above). We cut off the legs of the table to make it a comfortable height. Turn to page 143 for more information on this magical makeover.

It's easy to transform any bargain-priced hard-side suitcase into a delightful ottoman (right). Your choice of feet and cushion cover will make each one unique (see page 78 for a different look). Instructions are on page 143.

suitable foot

A dilapidated dresser or chest of drawers from the resale center can give rise to many creative projects. We wrapped batting and fabric around a thick foam pad and tucked it inside a dresser drawer. Classic turned wooden legs are simple to attach to your ottoman, adding height and understated elegance. Turn to page 144 for real prop-up-your-feet comfort!

It's fun and easy to transform flea market relics into conversation-starting ottomans. Here we simply added sturdy feet made from wooden post finials and used heavy webbed belting to attach a covered foam cushion (see page 143 for all the particulars). This well-traveled footrest is just the ticket for a trip down memory lane.

rest

LETTERS

MAIL

Mailbox #2-
#217

*Places in your heart.
A place for everything.
Boxes, bins, drawers, and tins —
reawakened, rearranged, and
ready for you to tuck away every
tiny treasure. With these chic and
trendy looks, it's the perfect time to*

Mailbox #2-
#217

GET ORGANIZED!

Functional and stylish storage can be yours — posthaste — with an inventive grouping of weather-worn mailboxes. You're sure to spot a variety of these relics at every flea market. Even the shabbiest examples can be easily brought back to life by applying a coat of off-white paint, followed by staining and wiping the surface to achieve an antiqued look. You might choose to paint your boxes in a variety of colors or finishes instead, or to apply metallic paints such as copper, bronze, or gold. It's all up to your imagination! Magazine-holder extensions on the mailboxes become handy hangers for umbrellas or outdoor garments. Put your stamp of approval on this weekend wonder — it's strictly first class!

... and everything

Your treasured collectibles deserve a setting as unique as they are! Collect old wooden crates and boxes that are about the same depth (our selection includes a divided silverware drawer organizer and a cheese box). If desired, stain the boxes to match, then place them in the most fitting arrangement and glue or screw together. To give your collector's shelf extra support, you may need to attach wooden laths or a piece of plywood cut to fit the size and shape of your finished shelf.

There's a place for everything, and everything in its place … whether you're organizing curiosities or correspondence, this old adage makes a lot of sense! You'll have your house neat and orderly in no time with nifty ideas like the handsome hideaway bins at right. To make them, simply paint old drawers (ours are wicker drawers from a baby's changing table) and then "antique" with gel stain. ⊕

in its place.

TREASURED TINS

You'd never want to tamper with the timeless beauty of collectible tins, but what about the stacks of ordinary boxes you see in resale shops? Try using scraps of embossed wallpaper to transform common tins into uncommonly beautiful canisters. In just one weekend, you can create an entire set of these attractive organizers, adding valuable storage space to any room!

There's a wealth of new wallpapers available that re-create the look of old-fashioned tin ceiling tiles. To "age" your wallpaper, follow the four easy steps below. Then use the paper to cover the sides of your tins. Top off your containers with a variety of finishes, such as covering the top with floral wallpaper and a glued-on trim. Or apply fresh coats of paint and crackle medium. Simple drawer knobs work great for feet, while vintage doorknobs make lovely handles.

Paint a piece of dimensional wallpaper with rust-colored acrylic paint and allow to dry.

Apply a coat of cream acrylic paint over the rust and allow to dry.

Lightly sand wallpaper to reveal spots of the underlying rust color.

Apply a coat of spray varnish, letting spray linger in some areas to create an aged look.

GET ORGANIZED!

TO THE
DESK
ADVANTAGE

Use your study to the "desk" advantage! Even if it's just a corner in the kitchen or den, the space in your home office can be maximized with attractive organizers.

Keep it all together with a handsome message center and storage boxes (opposite).

Perfect for holding current correspondence, the wooden "pocket" attached to our framed memo board is a drawer from an old-time sewing machine cabinet. We polished a cast-off frame to hold the fabric-covered insert, and the ribbon grid lets you post pictures and notes without pins. Old shirt buttons tack the ribbons in place. For the complete instructions, turn to page 144.

For a set of handy storage boxes, try wooden kitchen canisters. You may want to paint or stain your canisters if the finish is marred, or if it doesn't match your decor. All we did to ours was add knobs.

A deep wooden drawer gets a "lift" from wooden finials to become a helpful book or file box. Complete how-to's are on page 144.

young at art

Capture the imagination of a budding young artist with a private playground of practical-yet-fun finds refurbished in "palette-able" hues.

Stripes for a star on the rise: Want to refashion an old wooden desk into a youthful new workspace? See page 144 to brighten your desk with a little paint and striped fabric. If spills are a concern, cover your finished desktop with tempered glass. A purchased pair of pre-covered photo boxes tidies up the desk shelves. Cover the box lids with your leftover fabric scraps — decorating can be child's play!

Corkboard replaces the glass in a salvaged window, creating a fun bulletin board with versatile mini segments. Search the button box for multi-colored buttons and use jumbo push-pins to keep up with key items like notes, stickers, and jewelry. See the how-to's on page 145.

X O X O X O

IT'S ELEMENTARY: Chalkboard paint turns the sides of these flea market tins into writing surfaces. Top off the look by painting the lids with the same playful colors used on the desk and window. Apply primer to your tins before painting.

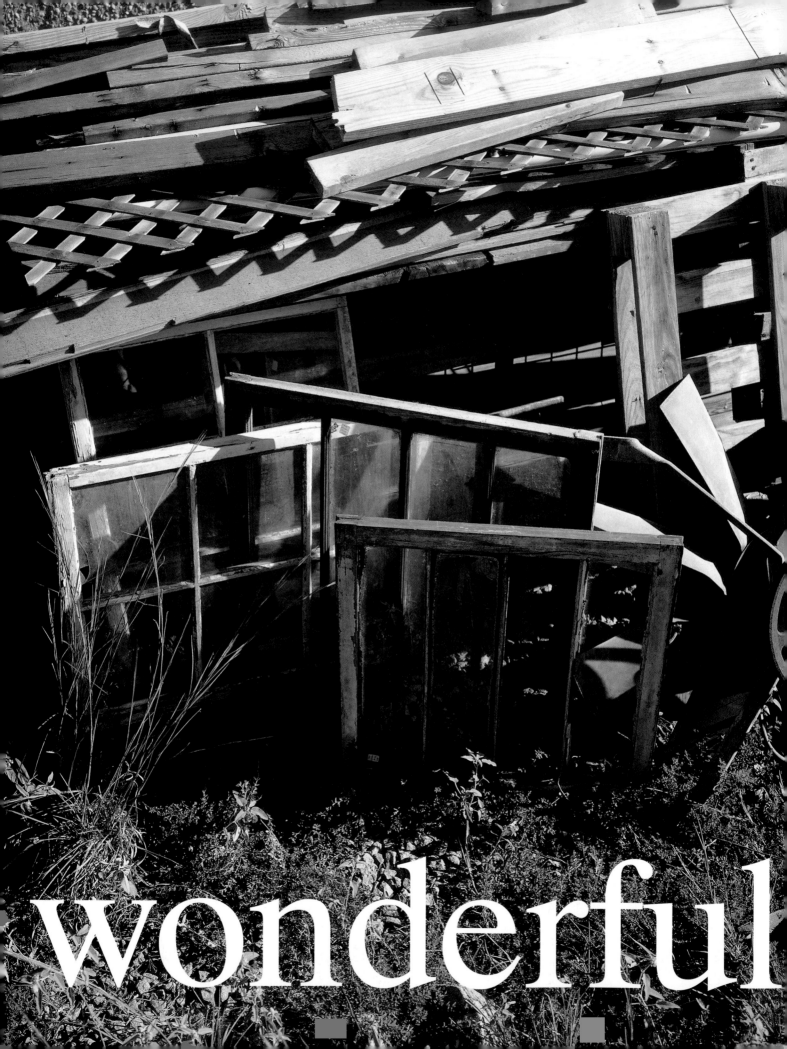

wonderful

Take a trip to any flea market or junk shop and you'll find a wealth of weathered windows, just waiting to be rescued! Once salvaged, they're easily transformed into decorative focal points or practical accessories, as you'll see on the following pages.

Proudly present Old Glory in an age-old window for all to see. Just follow our easy instructions on page 145 to enhance the frame's rustic look with a coat of whitewash; then paint our Colonial-style flag on the back of the glass panes, using masking tape to help you create uniform stripes. Attach wooden star cutouts to the front side of the glass to finish the patriotic look.

Even if a window has lost its glass, you can still find a way to make it useful. Why not turn it into a handy message center? We gave this one a fresh coat of white paint, then highlighted the panes with different colors on the inside edges. See page 145 for the instructions, including how to attach the cork board. ★

WINDOWS

a view with

If you don't have a flea market window, you can paint your faux stained glass pattern directly on an existing window of your home (just be sure your paint label says vertical application is possible). If you ever get tired of the design, you can easily change it. Simply remove the paint with a sharp craft knife or razor blade, peel off the leading, and start over with a new pattern.

a room

WINDOW ON HISTORY: Creating stained glass windows used to involve many hours of tedious work. Today, you can make a weathered window go from dull to dazzling in just one weekend. See page 145 for the pattern and instructions.

This door from a glass-fronted cabinet serves up bath linens on an old glass towel bar that we added. Drawer pulls became useful pegs when installed at either side of the doorknob. To sweeten the sentimental setting, we framed photocopies of three vintage valentines, provided on pages 154 and 155. Ribbons glued to the backs of the frames make hangers for these pretty pictures.

You can find oodles of old-fashioned costume jewelry and decorated hats at garage sales and flea markets for next to nothing! To make these beautiful frames, cover pre-cut mats with silk fabric scraps (see our basic instructions on page 146). Arrange bits and pieces of jewelry and hat trims as you please and glue in place. Easel backs, recycled from no-longer-used frames, make these new displays "stand" out.

frame of MIND

all in the

FAMILY

Your family is unforgettable — and your photo
gallery should be, too. Create striking memories
with framed silhouettes; page 147 shows an easy way
to make them using photographs. And don't
settle for ho-hum, everybody-has-them frames! Use
your imagination to create novel displays, such as
the plate frames shown opposite.

To showcase an heirloom photograph, trim a black-and-white photocopy to fit the center of a small dessert plate, then attach it with spray adhesive. Buy plate hangers or stands to display your unique frames.

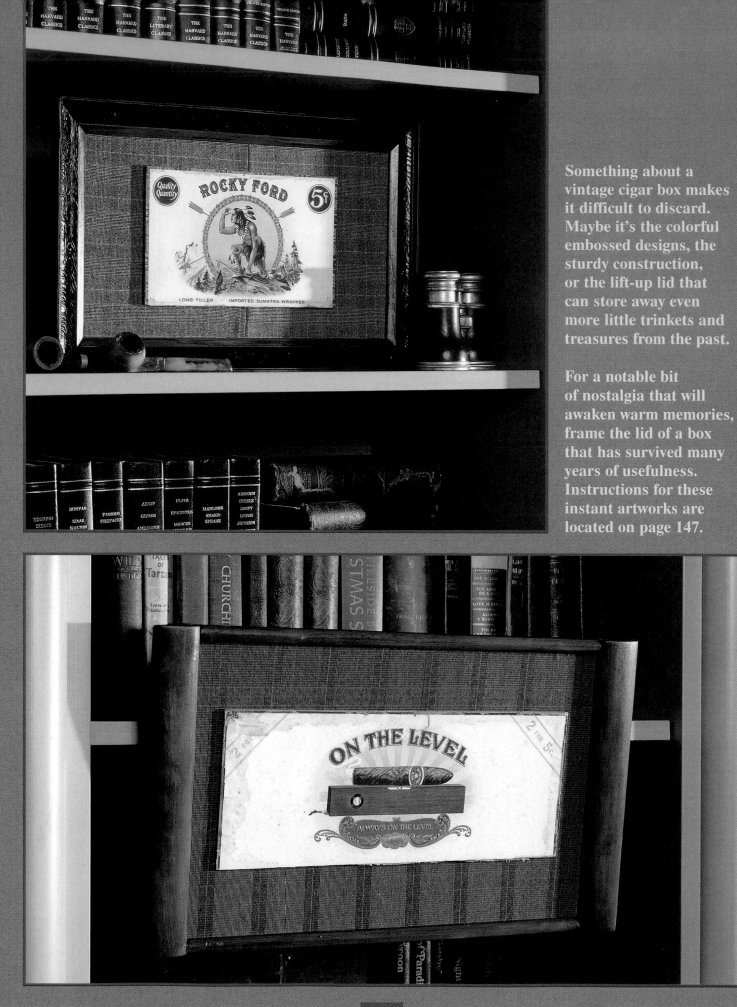

Something about a vintage cigar box makes it difficult to discard. Maybe it's the colorful embossed designs, the sturdy construction, or the lift-up lid that can store away even more little trinkets and treasures from the past.

For a notable bit of nostalgia that will awaken warm memories, frame the lid of a box that has survived many years of usefulness. Instructions for these instant artworks are located on page 147.

GENTLEMAN'S PREFERENCE

A tranquil corner can become a gentleman's sanctuary, a place where he can unwind in his own personal space.

Arrange a masculine wall grouping by dusting off some flea market frames and using them to display hallowed family photographs. Call some venerable neckwear out of retirement to display these worthy portraits. The simple transformation takes only minutes when you refer to the instructions on page 147.

CREATIVE

You'll find artworks in abundance at your local resale shop, making it easy to collect a variety of prints and paintings to suit your personal style. Our charming chickens are reproduction vintage prints we découpaged on pre-stretched art canvases. And don't let the simplicity of paint-by-number portraits blind you to their beauty. These playful pups and handsome hounds go together so well, you'd almost think they were litter mates.

To recreate these plucky prints, photocopy the designs on pages 156 and 157 and spray both sides with clear sealer. Découpage them onto pre-stretched canvases from a craft shop, and wipe on an aging glaze. Glue ribbon along the edges and cover the ribbon ends at top with a glued-on bow.

CANVASES

These faithful representations of man's best friend are just a few of the paint-by-number designs offered to the public in kit form over the years. After gluing them to pre-stretched canvases, paint the canvas edges to blend with the artwork. Fetching ceramic spaniels round out this canine collection.

It's an Ad, Ad, Ad World!

It's easy to "ad" a touch of 20th-century daily life to your kitchen. Advertisers have promoted their goods in magazines for decades, giving us a wealth of resources for fun works of art. You only have to visit a flea market or a pack rat's attic to find these memorable pages from the past, as well as the frames to hold them.

Some advertisements call for special treatment. To match the stainless-steel cabinets in a retro kitchen, this ad for an innovative line of break-resistant dinnerware needed a sleek metallic frame. Custom framing is worth the expense when the results are this satisfying!

Here's an idea that may help you when you're gathering framing materials: If you have the perfect ad but haven't yet found its frame, go ahead and have mats cut with 4" borders. When the right frame comes along, all you have to do is trim the mats to fit it. This flat wooden frame was a lucky find — with fabric strips glued on its borders, it coordinates perfectly with the ad and the mats.

Heart of the Home

RETRO RED — that's the cheery theme of this down-home kitchen. It's decorated entirely with pieces from the past. The bright canister set was a flea market find and so were the red teakettle and white milk glass tumblers. Clear glass bottles with apple-red labels make a nostalgic display on the windowsill. Crocheted doilies dainty-up the cabinet. The towel holder is made from a pot lid and a plate hanger, with ribbon forming the hanging loops for both the lid and the towel. Would you ever guess that the gingham-ruffled balloon shade began as a 1950's tablecloth? We tell how to take your linen from table to window via a quick makeover on page 141.

Looking for a way to use those wonderful glass jars you see in secondhand shops? Candles look great in any glass container and offer lots of decorator options. We used canning jars, a juice glass, a jelly jar, and a lidded refrigerator container for these pretty lights. To make your own poured candles, use candle-making supplies and follow the manufacturer's instructions.

An instant way to brew up a cozy mood with candlelight is to half-fill a jar with coffee beans, then settle a small vanilla candle into the beans. Remember, never leave any burning candle unattended!

Classy
GLASSES

Those bright-patterned juice glasses you've seen in flea markets have a history that's just as colorful. In the Depression years of the 1930's, certain manufacturers were looking for a new way to package their food products. They decided to try sturdy drinking glasses painted with gingham and flower designs. Thrifty housewives loved the pretty "freebies" that came with their jelly, cheese, or peanut butter and continued to favor them into the Fifties and Sixties. The designs painted on the glasses changed many times, but the quality of these little "Swigs" makes them just as desirable today as they were decades ago.

ALL SET TO GO:

These zesty-looking glasses sport the decorator colors of their era. Got a cool caddy full of matching tumblers? Fill them with flowers for an instant centerpiece. We've seen these portable beverage sets just about everywhere — a testament to their popularity!

SECOND HELPINGS

Set a terrific retro table with cool kitchen cloths from the mid-twentieth century, then cinch your dinner napkins with artistic Bakelite buckles. To fashion, thread a belt buckle onto the center of a length of ribbon. Wrap the ribbon ends loosely around the napkin, crossing in the back; thread ends back through buckle and knot the ribbon on top. To finish the scene, don't forget the daisies! The happy blooms echo the colors of the glassware set that holds them.

Convert an old pan lid into a towel holder — instantly! Just thread a sturdy ribbon through the lid handle, then tie the ribbon ends together to form a loop. Hang a classic kitchen towel through the loop ... your towel holder is ready for duty.

To hang your towel holder on the wall, use a plate hanger or glue a loop of wire to the back of the lid with silicone adhesive.

just-right blue & white

The classic combination of blue and white is always just right! We especially like to mix and match odd pieces of china — good buys on patterns from delftware to Blue Willow are easily found at flea markets, as well as inspiration on how to use your china finds. For instance, a broken-plate mosaic adds new character to a plain kitchen stool. On page 148, we share a foolproof technique for reassembling your china pieces in just the right order.

To make mosaic magic like this, sand, prime, and paint a kitchen stool, then dress up the seat with broken china pieces. The china-look details on the stool legs are strips cut from color photocopies of vintage print fabric, découpaged in place.

Dutch Treat

A collection of wooden shoes makes an interesting display — simply fill with sphagnum moss and tuck in faux flowering bulbs. To hang each shoe, nail a sawtooth picture hanger to the bottom of the heel or glue on a loop of wire.

The table's turned into a decorative asset

when you call upon an old-fashioned tablecloth to make your dining room furnishings coordinate. Simply use a color photocopier to duplicate the cloth on paper. Apply a clear spray sealer to both sides of the copy, then découpage the paper onto the tabletop and seal again to protect the surface. Our table was painted beforehand to complement the tablecloth colors.

Can't get enough of a favorite antique fabric? Without destroying a beloved vintage tablecloth or curtain, you can spread that marvelous pattern everywhere with color photocopies and découpage techniques! Over one weekend, you can turn a flea market table and a weathered bucket into harmonious accessories for your kitchen.

BLUE
PRINTS
❧ FOR ❧
HARMONY

To make this fun pail, prime and paint the sides of an old bucket and four wooden finials. Attach the finials to the bottom of the bucket for feet. Make color photocopies of the fabric motifs you wish to use, then cut the motifs from the copies — we cut leaves from plain white paper, as well. Apply clear spray sealer to both sides of the color motifs. Découpage the motifs to the sides of your bucket.

PUT A LID ON IT! Adopt some orphaned lids from your local flea market and put together a marvelous montage! Some lids are truly works of art, glazed and painted in a maze of intricate designs and colors. Clustered in a wall grouping, they're kaleidoscopic delights to the eye! To hang lids, attach loops of wire to the backs using silicone adhesive.

MORE TIME FOR OLD CHINA

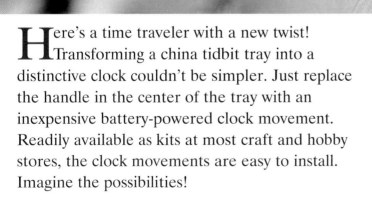

Here's a time traveler with a new twist! Transforming a china tidbit tray into a distinctive clock couldn't be simpler. Just replace the handle in the center of the tray with an inexpensive battery-powered clock movement. Readily available as kits at most craft and hobby stores, the clock movements are easy to install. Imagine the possibilities!

Your creation may be wall-mounted by using the hanger on the clock movement, or attractively displayed on a classic easel.

GOING FOR BROKE

Chipped plates and worn cabinets have more in common than just being bits of kitchen history. In the course of just one day, they can work together to provide you with many future years of service! After decades of hard use, the metal top on this charming old cabinet had finally rusted away. To create a coordinating mosaic countertop, we gathered several damaged china plates and broke them into pieces (turn to page 148 for our safety-minded technique). Remember to look at the back of your plates … if the manufacturer's marks are pretty or unusual, you may want to let them show.

Rye Grass

Cover the bottom of a watertight container with pebbles and top with at least 2" of soil. Sow rye grass seeds generously. Water with a spray bottle. Cover the container with plastic wrap and punch holes in the wrap to vent. Keep the soil moist and don't place in direct sunlight. When grass blades begin to emerge (about ten days), remove the wrap. In seven more days, your "lawn" will be ready to display!

*FRESH IDEAS: Pottery bowls and other
dishes are often the just-right fit in a decorator's
puzzle. The bowl resting atop our mosaic cabinet
is a natural choice for an easy — and fresh —
idea. Follow the rye grass recipe (opposite)
to grow your own indoor turf.*

GARDEN *fresh* STYLE

SAUCY BOUQUET: To delight passersby, use craft wire to hang a one-of-a-kind vase in the window. We used an old Worcestershire sauce bottle, but any small container with a ridged neck will work just fine.

No other season refreshes the soul like summer. After all, these are the months of budding flowers, games on the lawn, and kicking back in the shade. To make these memorable hours linger, surround yourself with some of the best elements of summers past.

Although it looks new, this durable glider is a well-weathered classic. It owes its fresh look to color-coordination and a little work done over just one weekend.

To revitalize a glider of your own, choose paint to match the fabric you will use on the cushion. Sand away the glider's rusty spots, then wipe off the dust with a tack cloth. Apply two coats of primer and two coats of your main color, then paint with the accent colors. Several coats of clear sealer will protect your glider's new finish.

To make the glider's comfy new cushion, cut a piece of thick foam to fit the seating area of the glider. Concealing the raw edges of the fabric, wrap the cushion gift-wrap style and hand stitch or safety pin the fabric in place.

sunny retreat

Pack up your picnic gear and bring it inside! A roomy secondhand basket inspired this indoor retreat filled with outdoor items. In fact, we've discovered that any alfresco article can enhance an "outside-in" decorating scheme.

OPPOSITE: Convert a pair of folding campstools into a fun and functional coffee table base. In just one weekend, you can paint the stool frames and make their new fabric seats! Using the original stool seat as a pattern, cut and hem a piece of fabric and tack it to the underside of the stool frame. Top the stools with a piece of tempered glass that has beveled edges. Cheery sunflowers are the natural choice to fill an insulated bottle "vase," and no campsite is complete without a graniteware coffeepot! ☀

> **A TIP FOR CUTTING CORNERS:** *Some textile mills offer pre-made pillows to coordinate with their fabrics, a great boon to busy decorators.*

TOP: For instant garden charm, frame a piece of fabric-covered mat board and glue on an enlarged photocopy of a vintage seed packet. BOTTOM: When it comes to organization, a big basket can make accessorizing a real picnic!

growing places

*To make a functional potting stand for an active gardener,
consider using a baker's rack from the flea market! Make it shady
by adding an easy-to-do canvas canopy. Get a piece of canvas that
fits around the top of the rack and use clear epoxy to quick-hem the
bottom edge. Then thread nylon cord through holes you've made in
the canvas along the top edge. Overlap the side edges at the back and
glue together. Pull the cording to gather the top of the canopy around
the baker's rack; tie the cord ends to secure. Stack enameled pans
and trays on the shelves, and this stand is open for business!*

HUMOR ON TAP: You'll hear a constant stream of chuckles with this wonderful waterworks of stacked enamelware. Refer to the diagram and how-to's on page 149 to assemble your fountain.

ENAMORED WITH
enamelware

Take it outside — your enamelware collection, that is. Those sturdy pans, plates, and pails are perfect for plenty of outdoor uses. With their no-nonsense finish, they can easily take any weather and look great doing it.

POUR ON THE CHARM: It doesn't have to be a vase — to be a vase! Any watertight vessel looks great when it's holding flowers … especially if it's a popular collectible like the enamelware pitcher shown opposite.

ONE COOL IDEA: A handy enamelware pail makes a curious ice bucket. Bring plenty of thirst-quenching summertime beverages to share — you never know who might drop in for a visit.

*W*ant a serene setting for your daybreak tête-à-têtes? Cover the lid of a standing sewing box with sheet moss and top with a circle of tempered glass, using self-adhesive surface protectors for no-slip stability — your table is ready! And the seating is just as easy with these wrought-iron chairs. Remove the padded seats and wrap them in fabric, stapling the edges underneath before replacing. You've just added a bit of garden freshness to your breakfast menu!

BREAKFAST

E P I P H A N Y

W̶ell...
Isn't this a
pretty pitcher!
COLLECTION!

Not sure how to display a special collection? Try arranging it on an unfamiliar framework —
you might just hit upon a grouping that professional designers would envy. Here, a weathered
flower cart shows off a baker's dozen of creamers in a monochromatic color scheme. Several had
distracting designs, but we just turned those to the back!

Garden Gatherings

orch, patio, veranda, sundeck, lanai … whatever you call your favorite outdoor space, it still means a place to unwind, relax, and shake off your daily cares. What better spot to display your collectibles than where you are totally at ease? And if your collection needs a little more climate control, you can always bring a bit of the outdoors inside. To make this cottage-cozy screen door display in just one weekend, turn to page 149. You'll feel right at home with your treasures presented so sweetly.

Flea market treasure hunters say it only takes three items to make a collection. With that in mind, this gathering of wicker "watering can" planters is growing very well.

how to do it...

Just follow these easy instructions and get the fuss-free, satisfying results you want!

Sparkling Conversation
Page 13

Hanging Beaded Vases and Candleholders

Make hanging beaded vases and candleholders by adding a beaded handle to the neck of a favorite glass jar or bottle.

Begin with a generous length of medium-gauge craft wire. Wrap one end of the wire around the top of the jar and twist the wire around itself to secure — form a handle and secure the remaining

wire end on the opposite side of the jar (cut excess wire from the end of the handle).

To decorate the handle, cut a piece of fine-gauge craft wire that is at least twice the length of the handle. Wrap one end of the wire around the top of the jar several times, adding beads as desired. Adding more beads as you go and ending at the opposite side of the handle, wrap the wire around the handle; twist the wire in place at the end of the handle and cut away excess.

To make a beaded dangle, loop and curl one end of a length of fine wire around the wires on the jar. Thread several beads onto the wire, then wrap the wire around and back through the last bead; twist to secure and cut excess.

To extend your decorative hanger, cut a piece of medium-gauge wire the desired length for the loop; cut a piece of fine-gauge wire twice as long. Adding beads to fine wire as desired, wrap the fine wire around the medium wire … twist the fine wire at opposite end and cut away the excess. Thread hanger through handle and twist ends at top to secure.

Time to Reflect
Page 16

Entryway Coatrack
Our entryway coatrack, shown above, may have originally been the mirrored top to a hutch or part of a mantel. When we

discovered it, the wood was in good shape, but the mirror was missing. We turned it upside down and realized it would make an attractive coatrack. To replace the missing mirror, we chose to add a decorator's touch by cutting a piece of mat board to fit the opening. We covered the mat board with a new fabric reminiscent of days gone by, then we inserted it into the opening and secured it in place with small finishing nails. Brass coat hooks, attached along the bottom edge, give new function to a unique find.

Tray Chic
Page 18

Cabinet Door Tray
Whether entertaining a crowd or just a few guests, our oversized serving tray, shown below, provides an elegant touch for your gathering. Your guests will be amazed to discover that this beautiful tray was once a kitchen cabinet door. After covering the door's recessed front panel with a wallpaper remnant, we glued split lengths of bamboo into the routed design which surrounds the panel (to keep bamboo strips from curling away from the tray's surface, place heavy books on the strips until the glue dries). All that was left to do was attach a stylish handle to each end of the tray and find the perfect tray stand or table to place it on. What a quick and easy gift idea for your friends who love to entertain!

TIP: We purchased our door prestained and varnished, but an unfinished door would work equally well. Simply sand the door, apply paint or stain, then finish with two coats of varnish.

TIP: If you don't have a wallpaper remnant, check out local stores for bargains. Retail stores often offer discontinued or sample wallpaper pieces at discounted prices.

results for any brand. One medium is applied between two layers of paint, a second is applied on top of two layers of paint (this is the medium we chose to create the effect shown at left), and a third crackle medium comes in colors that you apply over one layer of paint.

Round Trays 3 Ways
Page 22

Crackle-Finish Tray Table

To give our tray a timeworn finish, as shown above, we brushed on brown paint, then randomly sponged on black, before adding a crackle medium. Pieces of wicker-look fabric, cut to fit the shelves of an up-turned table, complete this fun and unique accessory.

TIP: Several types of crackle medium are available for your use; following the manufacturer's instructions will give you the best

Leopard Print Tray Table

This weekend, turn an old, scratched, or faded round metal tray into a modern decorator piece, like the one shown above. It's so quick and easy you may want to make another for a friend!

Apply primer to the tray. Paint the rim black and the center light beige ... more than one coat of paint may be necessary for even coverage.

To paint leopard spots, refer to the design on page 150, and paint brown dots in various sizes and shapes on the center of the tray — paint dark brown uneven lines along the edges of the spots. Apply a brown gel stain to the center of the tray, then wipe with a soft cloth to remove excess stain. Apply an antique metallic gold wax finish along the rim, then apply two coats of sealer to the entire tray. A perfect topper for an empty tray stand!

Tray Clock

For this timely French-inspired clock, place a round metal tray on a thick piece of wood, then drill a hole through the center to fit a purchased clock kit.

Paint the outside edges of the bottom of the tray ivory. Apply a clear spray sealer to the front and back of pages taken from old books. Applying glue only to the center of the tray, and overlapping and trimming as desired, follow découpage glue manufacturer's instructions to adhere pages to the center of the tray. Once glue is dry, use a craft

knife to trim the edges of the paper pieces even with the edges of the tray.

Make a photocopy of the clock face on page 151, enlarging or reducing it as necessary to fit your tray; cut out. Apply sealer to both sides of the photocopy. Découpage the clock face to the center of the tray.

To age the clock, apply a brown gel stain to the découpaged area on the clock, then wipe with a soft cloth to remove excess stain. Lightly spray clock with wood-tone spray. Apply a metallic bronze wax finish along the rim and the edges of the clock face ... seal with a clear varnish.

Follow manufacturer's instructions to assemble the clock movements on the tray (we purchased a set of longer hands to fit our clock).

I Remember
Page 27

Découpaged Verse Mantel

Give your fireplace a touch of romantic nostalgia with a refurbished wooden mantel. Paint the mantel to coordinate with your décor; paint the center panel off-white. Antiquing gel stain applied to the column turnings, top shelf, and edges of the panel adds an aged look to the new paint.

To embellish the center panel, make a color photocopy of the verse on pages 152 and 153 and apply a coat of sealer to both sides of the copies. Using a craft knife and cutting mat, cut out words individually, trimming as close as possible around each word.

For word placement on each line, make a straight guideline by placing a length of string across the panel and taping the ends. To center the verse, begin at the middle of the guideline and work toward each end of the panel, taping the words along the guideline. Repeat for second line. Once you are pleased with the placement of the verse, remove the guidelines. Use découpage glue to attach the words to the panel, removing the tape as you go. Once dry, apply two coats of découpage glue over the words to seal the verse.

I Remember
Page 27

Covered Chairs

Complementing our nostalgic mantel is a pair of straight-back chairs. After old padding and upholstery is removed, a little paint and stain on the elaborately carved backs helps the chairs coordinate with the mantel.
To pad each opening in the chairback and seat, use the existing fabric as a pattern to cut pieces of new fabric. Cut pieces of foam slightly smaller than the openings in the chair. For the front or the back of the chairback, staple one fabric piece over the opening and place the foam in the opening; staple the edges of the remaining fabric piece over the other side of the opening. Glue a decorative trim along the raw edges of each fabric piece.

TIP: To determine the thickness of the foam needed for your chair pads, measure the depth of the surrounding wood and double it.

Private Retreat
Page 28

Paneled Headboard and Footboard

To update the classic curves of this bed (below), we first cut patterns from kraft paper slightly smaller than the recessed areas of our headboard and footboard, allowing just enough room for our cording to fit around the panels. We added a new coat of paint to the areas that would show after we added the panels. We applied an antiquing stain, wiped away the excess stain, and finished with two coats of sealer.

Ordinary mat board is the base for the fabric-covered panels. Using the kraft paper patterns, cut shapes from the mat board and the batting ... cut fabric pieces one inch larger all around than the patterns. For each panel, center a batting piece, then a mat board piece on the wrong side of a fabric piece; fold and glue the edges of the fabric to the back of the mat board, easing it in place along the edges of the curves. Flanged cording glued along the edges of each panel adds an elegant finishing touch.
We glued the panels to the bed

using thick craft glue, then hammered finishing nails inconspicuously to the panels to secure in place.

Hearth to Headboard
Page 37

Firescreen Headboard

An easy-to-find flea market fireplace screen can be the focal point of your bedroom when made into a padded panel headboard (shown above); just cover mat board with batting and fabric to fit in the screen sections.

To make patterns for panels, lay each screen section down on kraft paper and draw along the inner edges. For each panel, use pattern to cut one piece each from mat board and felt; draw around the pattern on the batting and on the wrong side of the fabric ... cut out batting piece one inch outside and fabric piece two inches outside the drawn lines.

COVERING MAT BOARD OR CARDBOARD WITH FABRIC

Center batting, then mat board on wrong side of fabric; fold and glue edges of fabric to back of board.

For corners and curves, fold fabric to ease it in place and glue fabric to board.

To cover each panel, center batting piece, then mat board piece, on the wrong side of fabric piece; fold and glue the edges of the fabric to the back of the mat board, folding fabric to ease it in place along the edges of the curves. Glue the felt piece to the back of the panel, concealing fabric edges.

Finishing is a breeze! Just slip the fabric-covered panels under the edges of the metal frame … hot glue in place for a permanent decoration or use a needle and thread to tack panels to screen from the back for easy removal, so you can change panels with the seasons.

Beautiful Memories
Page 42

Elegant Candle

Turn forgotten "pearls" from old necklaces and bracelets into bright, beautiful candle adornments. To attach larger pearls, touch the tip of a low-temperature glue gun to the candle to melt a small "puddle" of wax and just press each pearl in place. Cover candle as desired with larger pearls. To fill the spaces in between and to "scatter" other pearls and seed beads, attach smaller pearls using $1/2$"-long gold sequin pins.

Favorite Columns for Light Reading
Page 54

Column Floor Lamp
You can build a column lamp (above) with an unlikely pair of flea market bargains. To give our simple lamp a solid base, we used the bottom half of an old wooden column. After cutting the column, we securely attached the bottom of the lamp to the top of the new base with silicone adhesive. We primed, then painted the entire lamp base. An antique finish was created by dry-brushing the surface with fruitwood gel stain. We draped strands of pearl beads from the top of a purchased shade and tacked in place, then trimmed with a row of delicate flowers removed from old hats. A clip-on earring makes a fancy finial addition.

Apple-Topped Topiary Lamp
To create an appealing lamp, like the one below, paint the column of a candlestick lamp dark brown. Sponge paint a small plastic urn with gold paint. Remove the base from the lamp if it is too large to fit in the urn. Place the lamp in the urn (for extra weight, add sand at the bottom of the urn … for extra height, add floral foam). Glue the lamp in the urn to secure.

For apple arrangement, cut a four-inch diameter plastic foam ball in half. Press ball halves around the top of the lamp to form the top of the topiary; glue halves together. Cut twigs to fit column of lamp; insert ends of twigs into bottom of foam ball; wrap and twist a length of craft wire around top and bottom of twigs to hold in place against lamp. Crisscross lengths of raffia around twigs to cover wire; tie ends of raffia together to secure. Glue moss over the ball, covering the ball completely; glue moss into the urn, covering the ends of the twigs. Dipping each pick into glue before inserting, cover the ball with miniature apple picks.

Cotton Comforts
Page 62

Pillowcase Partners
A pair of beautifully embroidered pillowcases team up to enhance a chairback and a small plain waste can.

To make the apron for the waste can, cut a strip from the decorative end of one pillowcase 1¹/₂" longer than the desired length. For flap, press raw edges of top of strip 1¹/₂" to the wrong side.

Use a seam ripper to open any seams in the remaining portion of the pillowcase. Measure the height of the waste can from rim to rim, then measure around the can and add one inch for overlap — cut a piece of poster board the determined measurement and cut a piece from leftover pillowcase slightly larger than the poster board piece. Using spray adhesive to attach, center and glue the poster board to the wrong side of the pillowcase piece, folding and gluing the edges of the pillowcase piece over

COVERING A CHAIR SEAT

Remove the seat from the chair. Draw around the seat on the wrong side of your fabric. Cut out fabric about four inches outside the drawn lines. Cut a piece of batting slightly smaller than fabric piece (you may want to cut several layers of batting for the desired thickness of your seat padding). Cut a piece of foam the same size as the seat. Layer the batting, foam, then the seat, at the center on the wrong side of the fabric.

Pulling the fabric taut, staple the center of opposite edges of fabric to the bottom of the seat. Working on opposite sides of the seat and stapling the edges in place as you go, stretch the fabric evenly around the seat, folding the fabric at the corners to ease in place. If necessary, trim excess fabric from bottom of seat. Reattach the seat to the chair.

the edges of the poster board. Overlapping ends at back, glue covered poster board to can. Measure around the can and add 10 inches; cut a length of 1" wide ribbon the determined measurement. Placing ribbon under the flap and knotting the ends at the back, attach the apron to the can.

For the chairback cover, determine the desired finished length for your cover, then double the measurement and add one inch. Cut across the second pillowcase, through both layers, at the determined measurement. Use fusible web tape to make a one inch hem along the raw edge. Press cover in half and place over chairback; sew buttons along the sides of the cover.

Vintage Embellishments
Page 66

Pillowcase Embellished Towel
Use a seam ripper to open the seams of an embroidered vintage pillowcase, then press the pillowcase flat. Measure the width of the towel and add 1"; cut a piece of lace the determined measurement, then cut a piece from the decorative end of the pillowcase the determined measurement by the width that you want it to be. Press the raw edges of the pillowcase piece $1/2$" to the wrong side; press the ends of the lace $1/2$" to the wrong side.

Placing the top edge of the lace across the long pressed edge of the pillowcase piece and folding the pressed ends of the lace to the back of the pillowcase piece, arrange the pillowcase piece and lace on the towel where it will be attached and pin in place. Sewing close to the top edges of the lace and pillowcase piece, sew in place.

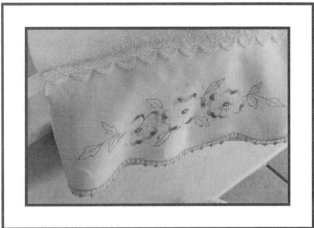

Beautiful Morning
Page 68

"Embroidered" Breakfast Tray

For an intriguing illusion, try this technique that uses a favorite doily without damaging it. At first glance, you can't tell that the doily we used on our embroidered tray isn't the real thing … it's a photocopy!

Paint your tray and a piece of cardboard cut a little larger than the doily the same color. Then use double-stick tape to hold your doily in place at the center of the painted cardboard. Make a color photocopy of the cardboard and doily. Trim close to the edges of the copied doily — the background color will blend in with the color of the tray, so you can avoid the risk of clipping your doily image by cutting too close. Découpage the photocopy to the center of the tray. Use paint pens with fine points to "embroider" running stitch bows and French knot and lazy daisy flowers on the tray. Apply two coats of sealer to the entire tray.

Remembrance
Page 70

Vintage Linen Accents

A great way to decorate sets of plain cards and envelopes is to add cutouts from color photocopies of embroidered linens, such as doilies and handkerchiefs. Trim a photocopy with decorative-edge scissors and use spray adhesive to attach it to a piece of scrapbook paper; trim the scrapbook paper piece to fit the front of a card or the flap of an envelope, for instance. Or use scrapbook paper as your card — fold and cut the paper piece to fit the envelope and then dress up the envelope by attaching a strip or two cut from a photocopied linen. The sky is the limit when duplicating the timeless beauty of vintage linens to mix with the stationery of today.

A corner cut from a handkerchief adds feminine charm to a purchased journal or address book. Since most handkerchiefs are sheer, simply cover the front with a glued-on piece of light-colored card stock cut slightly smaller than the piece of handkerchief or, if you desire, use decorative-edge scissors to cut the paper larger than the handkerchief, allowing the decorative edge to peek out from underneath. For a finished look on the inside of the cover, glue ribbon lengths over the raw edges of the handkerchief.

To make an heirloom keepsake, cut the decorative border from an embroidered pillowcase to accent an album. Center the decorative border on the front of the album, then fold and glue the raw edges to the inside; cover the raw edges with trim or ribbon lengths glued in place. We laced a coordinating ribbon through the eyelet closure of our envelope-style album.

Accents Made From Cheers Gone By
Page 73

Tablecloth Balloon Shade

A ruffled balloon shade made from a vintage tablecloth becomes the focal point for a retro-red kitchen.

To make the shade, measure the inside width of your window and multiply by two; measure the height of your window and add ten inches. If your tablecloth is close to this measurement, use it as it is, so you can avoid hemming the sides. Otherwise, cut your tablecloth the determined measurements and make a 1/2" hem along the side edges. Press the top edge of the tablecloth 4 1/4" to the wrong side; stitch across the top of the tablecloth 4" from the pressed edge; topstitch again at 2 1/2" from the pressed edge.

For the ruffle, measure the width of the shade and multiply by two; cut a piece of fabric this long by 5 1/2" wide, piecing as necessary. Make a 1/2" hem along one long edge (bottom) of ruffle. Baste 1/8" and 1/4" from the raw edge of the ruffle; pulling threads, gather the ruffle to fit the bottom edge of the shade. Matching the right sides and raw edges, pin the ruffle to the bottom edge of the shade; use a 1/2" seam allowance to sew the ruffle to the shade.

Insert tension rod through casing; mount rod at the top of your window, allowing 2" at top for the header. Cut two lengths of ribbon the length of the shade — drape ribbons over rod, around to the back of the shade, and pin or tie the ends together at the determined height to create balloon effect.

Have You Gone Mod?
Page 75

Polka Dot Painting Technique

To create a "spot-tacular" polka dot tray, spray your tray with primer. Paint the entire tray one solid color. Adhere several round stickers of one size randomly to the tray (making sure the sticker edges adhere). Paint the entire tray a second color. Place a few more round stickers of a different size on the tray and paint the entire tray with a third color. Repeat this technique as desired, varying the sizes of the stickers with each new color of paint (we used six colors on our tray). Using the tip of a craft knife, carefully remove the stickers from the tray. Spray the tray with two coats of sealer.

Ottoman Transition
Page 76

Sewing Machine Cover Ottoman

An antique wooden sewing machine cover with a flat top provides the base for the stylish yet easily constructed ottoman, shown above.

Cut a piece of thick foam to fit inside the top edges of the sewing machine cover; wrap foam with batting to soften the edges.

Place the wrapped foam on the cover. Center a piece of fabric over the foam. Folding and tucking in the corners, staple the fabric edges to the cover to secure in place (trim any excess fabric close to the staples). Glued-on decorative trim conceals the staples and the raw edges of the fabric, while nail-head trim adds a finishing touch.

TIP: Upholsterer's continuous nail-head trim, found in rolls at fabric or decorating stores, is a quick alternative to individual tacks.

MAKING A CUSHION WITH FOAM AND FABRIC

TIP: To cut through thick pieces of foam quickly and easily, use an electric knife.

To add stability to your cushion, you may want to add a piece of wood cut to fit the top of your project.

Center the batting, then the foam on the wrong side of a fabric piece cut large enough to cover the foam; place the wood piece on top. Wrap the edges of the batting over the foam and wood and staple in place. Wrap the fabric over the foam, folding the ends gift-wrap style and stapling in place as you go.

If you are covering the foam only, wrap the batting around the foam and then sew or safety pin the fabric in place at the bottom of the cushion. To create a nice finished edge, fold or press one long edge of your fabric to the wrong side before securing in place.

End Table Ottoman

Complete the end table ottoman (above) in no time at all. Cut a piece of plywood and thick foam to fit on the top of a discarded end table. Follow Making A Cushion with Foam and Fabric (opposite) to make a cushion for this new ottoman.

Timeworn Suitcase Ottoman

We refurbished our suitcase with a stylish, timeworn look that transcends the years.

Remove suitcase hinges and set the lid aside. Paint the suitcase bottom, then use an antiquing gel to stain it and the wooden post finials that will be used for feet. We found that dry-brushing the gel stain over the paint, then wiping the surface with a cloth, creates a soft, blended look.

To add the feet, cut a piece of plywood to fit in the bottom of the suitcase. Drill holes through the corners of the plywood and suitcase bottom. Screw the finials onto the bottom of the suitcase.

Turn the suitcase lid upside down and glue it to the top edge of the suitcase to create a recessed area for your cushion. Measure the height of the side of the lid from the trim to the top edge and double the measurement; measure around the lid and add one inch. Cut a strip of fabric the determined measurements. Matching wrong sides and long edges, press fabric strip in half; with pressed edge at bottom, glue along outside of lid just above the trim. Fold the raw edges to the inside and glue in place.

A piece of thick foam, cut to fit and covered with fabric, can be inserted into the lid to complete the ottoman.

TIP: Painting your suitcase a neutral shades and using a neutral fabric trim will allow you to change the fabric of the cushion as your décor changes.

Suitable Footrest,
Page 78

Belted Suitcase Ottoman

By adding "feet" to the bottom of an old suitcase and a fabric-covered foam piece to the top, you can create an ottoman in just a couple of hours. We reinforced the bottom of the suitcase with a piece of plywood before adding large post finials, stained to match, to the bottom corners. Strap your cushion in place by gluing or stapling the ends of the webbed belting lengths to the bottom of the ottoman.

Suitable Footrest
Page 79

Drawer Ottoman

Don't throw that drawer away … quick as a wink, you can turn it into a unique ottoman — see above. Refinish the surface of the drawer with a timeworn painting technique and add matching wooden screw-in legs and new drawer pulls … start with a dark base coat, paint a light top coat, then lightly glaze with a glossy wood-tone spray; sand randomly to reveal underlying colors of paint. To complete this footstool, place thick foam in drawer for height, then top it with another piece of thick foam covered with fabric. For how-to's on covering foam, see page 142.

To the Desk Advantage
Page 86

Message Center

Combine a found sewing machine drawer with a flea market picture frame to make this fabulous message center (shown right) in just one afternoon! For memo board, cut a piece of foam core board and batting to fit in the frame; cut a piece of fabric one inch larger on all sides than the foam core. Place the fabric piece, wrong side up, on a flat surface; layer the batting, then the foam core at the center of fabric piece, then fold and glue fabric edges to the back of the foam core. On front of memo board, use lengths of grosgrain ribbon to shape evenly spaced diamonds, gluing the ends to the back of the board. Use a heavy-duty needle and thread to sew buttons at each intersection of ribbon, going through all layers. Mount the memo board in the frame.

Stain the sewing machine drawer to match the frame. To make a backing, place the frame on one long edge of the drawer, and measure the height of the drawer and frame; measure the width of the frame. Cut a piece of mat board the determined measurements; use small brads, tacks, or hot glue to attach mat board to back of the frame and drawer.

Book Drawer

Turn that too-good-to-resist flea market drawer (shown above) into a trendy necessity for your den … in only an hour or two! Stain four wooden finials plus all surfaces, inside and out, of the drawer to match your drawer front. If necessary, reinforce the corners of your drawer with wood blocks. Use wood glue or screws to attach finials to the bottom corners of the drawer.

Young at Art
Page 88

Fabric-Covered Desk

Give a salvaged desk a modern look any person would be proud to show off. Paint the entire desk a favorite color. Be creative and have fun painting the rungs of the legs in accent colors that match your fabric or décor.

Select a coordinating fabric to cover the top of the desk and the front of any drawers. Cut a piece

Paint remaining exposed glass red. Don't worry about painting "outside the lines"; the edges of the red stripes will be concealed behind the white. Paint wooden stars gold, dry brush them with white paint, then glue them to the front of the blue pane using silicone adhesive.

Window Bulletin Board

What can you do with an old wooden window once the glass is broken? Turn it into a handy accessory for your child's room. Paint around the inside edges of each pane section with a different color. For each section of memo board, cut a piece from rolled cork and foam core board to fit inside the pane. Use spray adhesive to attach cork pieces to foam core pieces ... secure memo boards into panes with glazier points or tacks. For backing on the entire window, cut a piece of mat board slightly smaller than the window. Glue and/or nail the backing to the window.

View with a Room
Page 92

Faux Stained-Glass Window

Turn a castaway window frame into a unique art piece in no time at all using simulated leading and acrylic glass paints. For your window, trace the pattern, page 155, onto tracing paper, then tape the pattern to the front of the window (reduce or enlarge pattern on a photocopier if needed to fit your window, then tape photocopied pattern to the window). On the back of the glass, use a dry-erase pen to draw over the pattern lines and to freehand draw additional designs. Following the manufacturer's instructions, apply self-adhesive lead strips on the front of the glass over the outlines. Follow manufacturer's instructions to paint the design with glass paint.

Don't forget to remove the marked lines from the back of your window before you show it off!

of fabric large enough to cover each area and wrap around the edges. Fold under raw edges and staple to the wood.

Wonderful Windows
Page 91

Americana Flag Window

What better way to show your American pride than with a red, white, and blue window? Use a weathered wooden frame as is or whitewash it to add rustic charm. Working on the back of the window glass, paint the top left pane blue ... use painter's masking tape to mask off equal-width stripes on the remaining panes; paint the exposed glass white, then remove the tape.

View with a Room
Page 93

Towel Bar Window

Our framed valentines add an air of romance to this simple window towel bar (above). Using white card stock, make color photocopies of the vintage prints on pages 154 and 155, enlarging or reducing as needed to fit in your frames. Cut the images out along the edges.

Our three found frames add shimmer with a touch-up of gold paint. For a background, we chose to glue our valentines onto a piece of mat board that was cut to fit each frame. Silky ribbons tied into bows, with their ends glued to the backs of the frames, make dainty hangers — display the framed valentines from knobs added to a glass-front cabinet door.

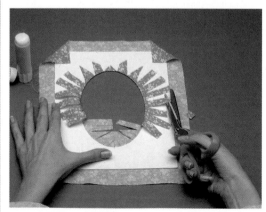

Frame of Mind
Page 95

COVERING A PRE-CUT MAT

When covering a pre-cut mat board with fabric, you can use several methods to attach the fabric ... fusible web is tried and true, while spray adhesive can also be quick and easy. A craft glue stick, as we have shown, is one way to tack the raw edges to the back of the frame.

Cut a piece of fabric an inch larger all around than your pre-cut mat board. Adhere front of mat at center on wrong side of fabric piece and draw around center cutout. Use a ruler to mark the cutting lines for the cutout area (opening) of the mat. For a rectangular mat, draw an X from corner to corner — for an oval, draw center lines vertically and horizontally, then draw horizontal lines at half-inch intervals through the middle of the oval. At the top and bottom of the oval, draw cutting lines at an angle to ease the fabric around the curves of the mat. Using a craft knife and a cutting mat, cut along drawn lines to within $1/8$" of edges of opening.

Spray adhesive on front of mat; center mat on wrong side of fabric. Cut ends of fabric pieces to fit back of mat; fold, then glue fabric to the back of the mat.

Fold fabric corners diagonally over corners of mat and glue in place. Fold outer fabric edges to back of mat, smoothing fabric and gluing in place.

All in the Family
Page 96

Framed Silhouettes

Coupled with frames we unearthed at a collector's market, these silhouettes, shown below, will become the heirlooms of tomorrow. A coat of black paint creates a dramatic finish for a gold plastic frame; after the paint is dry, apply a metallic gold wax buffing compound over the decorative border.

To turn a side-view portrait into a silhouette, photocopy the photograph you wish to use (enlarging or reducing it as necessary to fit in your frame). Using repositionable adhesive, attach the photocopy to the back (white side) of the silhouette paper, then, using small scissors, carefully cut out the silhouette; cut a curved edge along the bottom of the silhouette to give it a finished look. Use spray adhesive to attach the silhouette to background paper that has been cut to fit inside your frame.

TIP: The best photograph for a silhouette is a clear profile with sharp edges. When taking the picture, position the subject four to five feet in front of a plain background, light them from behind, and do not use a flash. The finished silhouette will be in reverse from the original photo; either reverse the person's pose or reverse the photo on a photocopier.

TIP: If there are details on your silhouette that are too small to cut out accurately, use a black permanent pen to draw in the details on the background paper after the silhouette is glued down.

Gentleman's Preference
Page 96

Framed Cigar Box Lids

For collectibles with masculine appeal, try unusual displays such as our framed cigar box lids (left). Cut a mat board insert to fit your frame, then cut fabric from the back of a men's vintage suit jacket and glue it to the mat; glue the cigar box to the center of the mat. A refurbished flea market frame or a no-longer used wooden tray adds a gentlemanly touch to this instant project.

Small Frames & Bow Tie Hangers

Your ancestors never looked better ... men's vintage clip-on bow ties, classically ornate wooden frames, and treasured photographs can come together in a unique family display. For each hanger, use a piece of ribbon or old belting and glue one end to the back of a bow tie ... glue the other end to the back of the frame. To hang the frame, tack to the wall using a small nail hidden underneath the center of the bow tie.

TIP: Straight pins make wonderful hangers for lightweight objects. Simply tap the head of the pin with a hammer (using two pins at once makes a stronger hanger). When removing the hanger later, simply smooth over the tiny hole with a finger — hardly noticeable!

Just Right Blue & White
Page 110

China Mosaic Stool

To make a china mosaic stool like the one above, choose a plate that is slightly smaller than the seat of your stool. Cut a piece of clear self-adhesive vinyl larger than your plate. Remove the paper backing from the vinyl and smooth the adhesive side onto the back of the plate, taking care to remove as many air bubbles as possible.

Place plate upside down between layers of a towel.

Use a rubber mallet to break the plate into pieces — if some pieces are larger than you want, replace the towel over the plate and hit the pieces again with the mallet.

Carefully remove the towel and turn the plate right side up, leaving the vinyl intact — discard any pieces that are too small to use.

Beginning at the center, peel the broken plate pieces from the self-adhesive vinyl and arrange them on the top of the stool; sand any sharp areas on the plate pieces. When satisfied with your mosaic design, use tile adhesive to glue the pieces in place on the stool, following the manufacturer's suggested drying time.

Apply and smooth tile grout around the mosaic pieces and along the edges of the seat, following the grout manufacturer's instructions. Sand any remaining sharp areas on the mosaic pieces and any rough spots on the grout. Apply several coats of clear sealer to the stool.

Going for Broke
Page 117

Mosaic-Topped Cabinet

We left this rustic cabinet (above) as we found it, choosing only to refurbish its top with a china mosaic that coordinates with the color of the cabinet.

Start by cleaning, sanding, and priming your cabinet top. Place each china plate upside down between the layers of a towel and use a mallet to break it into pieces. Remove the china pieces from the towel … if any piece is larger than you want, replace the piece between the layers of the towel and hit it again with the mallet. Carefully discard pieces that are too small to use. Sand any sharp areas on the plate pieces.

Working from the center out, use tile adhesive to glue the broken pieces to the cabinet top and follow the manufacturer's suggested drying time.

Follow the grout application instructions for the China Mosaic Stool (page 148) to finish the cabinet.

Enamored with Enamelware
Page 125

Dishpan Fountain

To make a dishpan fountain like the one above, you will need to use ¹/₂" diameter galvanized plumbing pieces throughout: 4"-long nipples, four 90° elbows, one lavatory faucet, one female straight connector, one hose barb, one nipple the desired height for your fountain, and an indoor/outdoor fountain pump that is the size needed to operate your fountain.

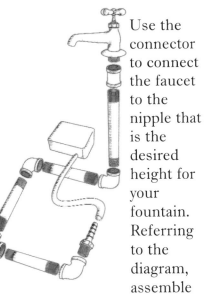

Use the connector to connect the faucet to the nipple that is the desired height for your fountain. Referring to the diagram, assemble the remaining nipples and elbows into a freestanding base for your faucet; thread the hose barb into the last elbow. Position the faucet base in the dishpan.

Follow the fountain pump manufacturer's instructions to install pump in bottom of pan and to connect plastic tubing to hose barb. Fill the bottom of the pan with rocks for weight … and arrange your enamelware pieces in the pan until they provide the most pleasing sound of trickling water.

TIP: If you're making your fountain a permanent fixture, use clear silicone sealer to glue your dishware pieces in place.

Garden Gatherings
Page 130

Screen Door Corner Display

In just one weekend, you can make an "a-door-able" display unit by hinging two wooden screen doors together (see above). Attaching ribbon lengths in a lattice pattern makes a unique way to display old postcards and photos. Carefully remove the wooden trim around the frame of the door where you wish to make your lattice design. Glue or staple the ends of the lengths of ribbon to the door to hold in place until you reattach the trim. Using a heavy-duty needle and thread or lengths of wire, sew buttons to the screen through the ribbons at each overlap.

Use recycled brackets and old drawer fronts to add shelves for your favorite knickknacks. Hang a hat or a threesome of plates and fasten on a tension rod for a delicate valance, and you will have created the perfect presentation for your treasures!

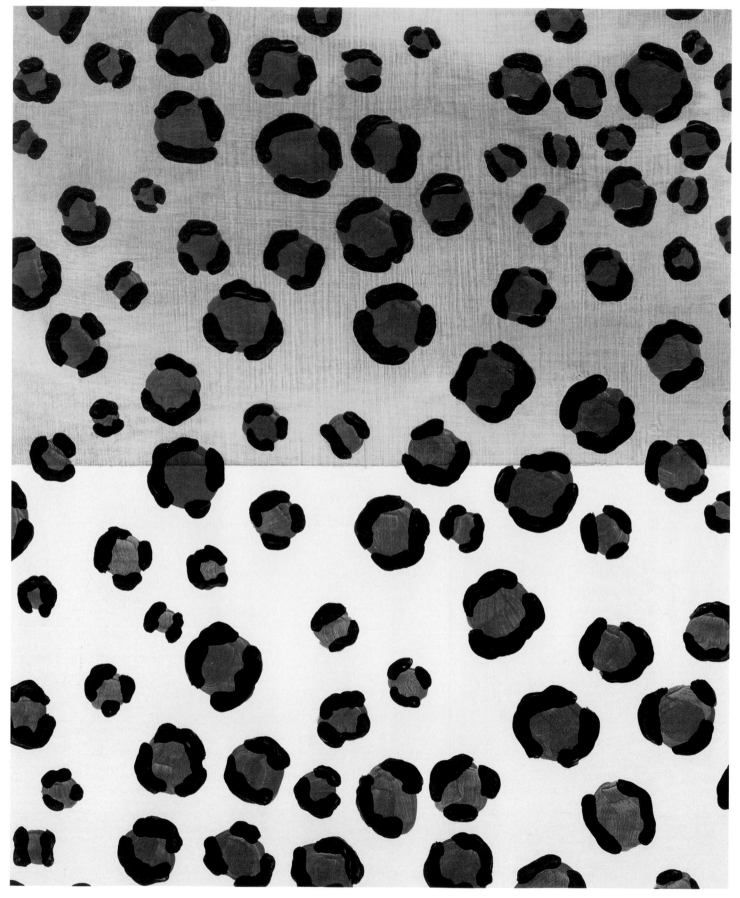

Découpaged Verse Mantel, Page 135

I remember,
I remember,
The house where
I was born,

The little window · where the sun · came peeping in · at morn.

First Impressions, Page 9

Reduce or enlarge pattern at a copy shop as needed to fit your sign.

Towel Bar Window, Page 146

A Token of Love

Faux Stained-Glass Window, Page 145

For a whole tulip pattern, fold a tracing paper piece in half. Place the folded edge along the straight line of the half-tulip pattern and draw over the pattern lines; turn paper over and draw over traced lines. Unfold paper and draw a line along fold from top to bottom to complete tulip pattern.

MR E. TUDMAN'S PARTRIDGE COCHIN HEN

"TITANIA"

FIRST PRIZE AT BIRMINGHAM IN 1870 AND 1871.

A. Goater, Nottingham.

where to find it

Pages 74/75
Have You Gone Mod?

Floor Pillows:
Trim
Manufactured by
Hollywood Trims®

Pages 78/79
Ottoman Transitions

**Sewing Machine
Cover Ottoman:**
Nail-head trim
Manufactured by
Massasoit/Tackband, Inc.

**Timeworn Suitcase
Ottoman:**
Stripe fabric
Manufactured by
Shabby Chic®

Gel Stain
Fruitwood
Manufactured by
Delta Ceramcoat®

Pages 86/87
To the Desk Advantage

Message Center:
Ribbon
Manufactured by
C.M. Offray & Son, Inc.®

Pages 92/93
A View with a Room

**Faux Stained-Glass
Window:**
Glass painting supplies
Manufactured by
Gallery Glass®

Pages 112/113
Blue Prints for Harmony

**Découpaged Bucket
and Table:**
Decoupage glue
Manufactured by Anita's™

Pages 114/115
More Time for Old China

Tidbit Tray Clocks:
Clock movements
Manufactured by
Walnut Hollow®

Pages 128/129
Breakfast Epiphany

Table and Chairs:
Chair seat fabric
Manufactured by
Shabby Chic®

Page 130
Garden Gatherings

Screen Door Display:
Window valance
Manufactured by
Peking Handicrafts

MANUFACTURERS

American Art Clay Co., Inc.
Rub 'n Buff®
717 W. 16th Street
Indianapolis, IN 46202
1-800-374-1600
www.amaco.com

Anita's™
Back Street, Inc.
3270 Summit Ridge Pkwy NW
Suite 200
Duluth, GA 30096
www.backstreetcrafts.com

C.M. Offray & Son, Inc.
857 Willow Circle
Hagerstown, MD 21740
1-800-344-5533
www.offray.com

Conso®
Conso International, Inc.
P.O. Box 326
513 North Duncan By-Pass
Union, SC 29379
1-800-845-2431
www.conso.com

Delta Ceramcoat®
Delta Technical Coatings, Inc.
2550 Pellissier Place
Whittier, CA 90601
1-800-423-4135

Design Master®
Design Master Color Tool, Inc.
Box 601
Boulder, CO 80306
(303) 443-5214
www.dmcolor.com

Eclectic Products, Inc.
1075 Arrowsmith Street
Eugene, OR 97402
1-800-693-4667
1-541-746-2217

Gallery Glass®
Plaid® Enterprises, Inc.
3225 Westech Dr.
Norcross, GA 30092-3500
1-800-842-4197
www.plaidonline.com

Hollywood Lights™
Wisconsin Lighting, Inc.
800 Wisconsin Street,
Suite D02-104
Eau Claire, WI 54703
1-715-834-8707
www.wilighting.com

Hollywood Trims®
Prym-Dritz Corp.
P.O. Box 5028
Spartanburg, SC 29304
1-800-845-4948
www.dritz.com

Hot Off The Press, Inc.
1250 NW Third
Canby, OR 97013
1-800-227-9595
1-888-326-7255
www.hotp.com

Krylon®
The Sherwin-Williams Co.
101 Prospect Ave. N.W.
Cleveland, OH 44115
1-800-457-9566
www.krylon.com

Lion Ribbon Co.
C.M. Offray & Son, Inc.
Rt. 24, Box 601
Chester, NJ 07930
1-908-879-4700
www.offray.com

Martha Stewart
everyday colors™
Martha Stewart Living
Omnimedia, Inc.
20 West 43rd Street
New York, NY 10036
1-800-950-7150
www.marthastewart.com

Massasoit/Tackband, Inc.
118 Dulong Circle
Chicopee, MA 01022
1-800-523-0017
1-413-593-6731
www.tackband.com

Minwax®
The Sherwin-Williams Co.
101 Prospect Ave. N.W.
Cleveland, OH 44115
1-800-523-9299
www.minwax.com

Mona Lisa Products
Houston Art, Inc.
10770 Moss Ridge Road
Houston, TX 77043-1175
1-800-272-3804
www.houstonart.com

Peking Handicrafts
1388 San Mateo Ave.
So. San Francisco, CA 94080
1-650-871-3788

Ralph Lauren Paint™
Polo Ralph Lauren Corp.
New York, NY 10022
1-888-475-7646
www.polo.com

Shabby Chic®
Fashion Island,
Newport Beach
571 Newport Center Drive
Newport Beach, CA 92660
949-219-0663
www.shabbychic.com

Walnut Hollow®
Walnut Hollow Farm, Inc.
1409 State Road 23
Dodgeville, WI 53533
1-800-950-5101
www.walnuthollow.com

Wrights®
West Warren, MA 01092
1-597-877-4448
1-800-628-9362
www.wrights.com

Any supplies not listed here
can usually be found at craft
stores or hobby shops.

hats off to...

Photography Stylist: Becky Charton

Photographer: Mark Mathews, The Peerless Group,
Little Rock, Arkansas

Our sincere appreciation goes to the following businesses for
their contributions to this book: Argenta Antique Mall, 201
East Broadway, North Little Rock, Arkansas 72114; European
Gifts & Home Furnishings, 5100 Kavanaugh Boulevard,
Little Rock, Arkansas 72207; and Collector's Market, 22430
Interstate 30, Exit 123, Bryant, Arkansas 72089.

We would also like to extend a warm *thank you* to the generous
people who allowed us to photograph in their homes: Belinda
Brolo, Debbie Denton, Melissa Fowler, Chris Ham, September
Hearen, Courtney Henry, Mark Mathews, Frankie McKay,
Ellison Poe, Susan Reynolds, and Layton Weeks.

We also say *thanks* to Cynthia Sumner for sharing her china plate
border idea shown on page 12.

*And our special thanks go to you for adding this labor of love
to your library. It is our sincere hope that this book has provided
you with creative inspiration and greater enjoyment of the flea
market experience.*